risk a verse:
A YEAR IN
DAILY SONNETS

LIBBY WEBER

BURRITO BOOKS | SAN DEIGO

Burrito Books
San Diego, CA
www.burritobooks.com

Cover photograph: Bonjwing Lee ©2017
Cover design: Patrick "Pup Atlas" Bowman and Az Klymiuk ©2018
Author photograph: Weston Bennett ©2017
Poetics Book Layout: Book DesignTemplates.com ©2017

Publisher's Cataloging-in-Publication data

Names: Weber, Libby, author.
Title: Risk a Verse: A Year in Daily Sonnets / by Libby Weber
Description: First trade paperback edition
San Diego: Burrito Books, 2018
ISBN 978-0-692-96045-5

For Jeff

That will be my memorial,
not stone, not ash,
but one damned poem after another.

–JANE YOLEN

Contents

Introduction

I don't remember precisely what sparked my decision to write a sonnet every day for a year. It's probable that nothing did—it was just an idea that occurred to me when I was chatting with my friend Sara. Fortunately, one of Sara's many fine qualities is a certain willingness to entertain and encourage ambitious and/or ridiculous ideas. Regardless of what random neurons fired to create the idea, this is how it went from thought to project:

"Should I write a sonnet every day next year?" I asked.

"If you don't, I will never speak to you again."

And that was pretty much it.

Of course, the decision was hardly irrevocable. I wibbled, as is my wont. Having a big idea is easy. Convincing yourself to take on a writing project of unprecedented scope, despite numerous other commitments, is more challenging. However, the more people I talked to, the more encouragement I got. Eventually, I wrote Sara an e-mail with the subject, "Shit, I really have to do this, don't I?"

So I did.

The rules I set for myself were simple: write a sonnet every day for a full calendar year. No writing ahead. No skipping days. No "Sleep now, I'll write in the morning." Every day, I had to make enough time to write a fourteen-line poem that rhymed and scanned and post it online, which I hoped would keep me honest and serve as sufficient motivation not to write "Ba-DUM ba-DUM ba-DUM ba-DUM ba-DUM" for fourteen lines.

Of course, I had other goals in mind, namely to make an earnest attempt to capture each day and the things I was doing and thinking about. I knew I had some exciting upcoming things that would make interesting sonnet subjects, like my annual writing retreat, singing with the San Diego Symphony and San Diego Opera, and sharing the stage with folk-rock legends the Indigo Girls.

What I hadn't anticipated was the way the daily sonnets encouraged me to jump at interesting performance opportunities that came my way, which is how I ended up as part of the US premiere of a musical based on Disney's *The Hunchback of Notre Dame* and got to sing Michael Giacchino's score for *Star Trek (2009)* live with a showing of the film. Unsurprisingly, I also managed to get a tad overscheduled, which is why there are so many sonnets about being exhausted ("Yay," April 28th).

I like to think I went in to the project with ample knowledge and preparation. I love to read, and I've been writing rhyming verse since I childhood, so it feels quite natural to me. My parents instilled a love of poetry at an early age—I recall being read works by Edgar Allen Poe, Shel Silverstein, Christina Rossetti, William Blake, James Whitcomb Riley, and many others, and I fell deeply in love with Shakespeare when I was a teenager at integrated arts camp. (Yes, I went to integrated arts camp. Shut up. It was awesome.) When I returned to my hometown in rural Illinois, I co-founded a creative writing club at my high school, and later learned the proper names for things like heroic couplets and scansion while studying reading and writing poetry in college. In subsequent years, my verse writing developed from an entertaining way to pass the time into a staple of my creative and professional writing. So in my mind, I'd been in training to write daily sonnets for years. However, I soon came to realize that this was overstating the case somewhat.

One could generously characterize my decision not to do any warm-up sonnets in the weeks preceding New Year's Day as confidence. One could also call it hubris. I knew I was perfectly capble of writing a sonnet every day. However, I also wanted to make them good, and a few practice sonnets might have saved me from some of the mistakes I made early on, like taking on a concept that was too ambitious or overly twee ("Onomatopoeia Sonnet," January 5th), blurring the line between parody and homage ("Mising Leter Sonet," January 3rd), or forcing myself to write an idea in which I had decreasing confidence ("An Italian-ish Sonnet Inspired by Austrian Music," January 18th) instead of just scrapping the idea and writing something different. On the other hand, I rather like some of the sonnets that resulted from being dissatisfied with my own work ("Meh," January 16th).

I also ended up fudging some of the rules along the way. To be fair, some of them were arbitrary, like wanting to remain politically neutral at all times, no matter how dramatic world events were, in an attempt to keep the sonnets from feeling dated. Fortunately, I figured out that this was a pointless rule and broke it on several occasions ("Ferguson," August 19th; "Hopeless," November 6th). I also quickly realized that there was no way I was going to keep to my initial idea of writing a sonnet a "day" between midnight and midnight of any given date. When you work an eight-hour work day followed by a three-hour rehearsal and have other writing and music to work on, it can be tough to find time to write a sonnet until right before bed. That usually means staying up until after midnight to finish. Thus "day" became "waking hours," and I was much happier for it, if sleep-deprived. Of course, even that didn't save me from the time that I wrote the day's sonnet, saved it as a draft, and didn't realize I hadn't published it until several days later ("Luxury of Laps," August 3rd). Fortunately, WordPress lets you backdate entries (and *mea culpas*). Writing daily sonnets was nothing if not an exercise in forgiving myself for imperfections and moving on.

If you compare the sonnets in this book to the versions that were published online, you will notice that not only have these sonnets been annotated for context and to cite literary and cultural references, but also that errors like missing words and extra metrical feet have been corrected. I did preserve the sonnets' original end rhymes, forms, and concepts in an attempt to compromise the desire to be honest presenting this as the work I did during the year with the desire to provide readers with technically and grammatically sound sonnets. I'm definitely not trying to hide the fact that I wrote a sonnet with a penis joke in every line ("An Extremely Juvenile Sonnet," April 14th), I merely wish to provide the reader with the finest penis-joke sonnet reading experience possible.

As I prepared this collection for publication, I was reminded of looking through a box of family photos from before the days of digital cameras. Before you could check the shot and retake or retouch those with which you were dissatisfied, you saved whatever recognizable shots you managed to capture, since those were your only artifacts of the experience. And since you paid to have all of them developed, you kept them, even the ones where Little Sally got her hands on the camera and took a series of up-the-nose pictures. Or, in my case, sonnets which I typed up with one hand for thematic reasons ("Left-Handed Compliments," May 17th). And sometimes, those become your favorite pictures.

But, like family snapshots, sometimes even the silly ones are part of a bigger story, one that's perhaps different from the one you think you're telling when you make it. When I read these sonnets, I see the desire to put messy, complicated experiences into some sort of frame, be it poetical or narrative. Life, of course, resisted, but that didn't stop me from trying to spin a bit of spray-paint in the parking lot into life advice ("Be Happy," January 23rd) or imagining that all of my daydreams of being able to quit my day job ("Fishing," May 8th) would somehow be realized during the year because I was opening myself to the universe ("Positive Reinforcement," June 2nd). And while I may still be working my day job at the time I publish this book, I'm still singing, I'm still writing, and my life is still being enriched by the stories that started, continued, and ended while I was sonneting daily. And I still write down the things that catch my eye or stick in my mind. I look forward to finding out what final form those experiences take. Even the penis jokes. Especially the penis jokes.

San Diego

September 20th, 2017

What is a sonnet, anyway?

Sonnet form, as you'll read in "Sonnet 101" (January 1st), is simple. A sonnet is a poem comprised of fourteen lines in deliberate rhyme and meter. There is also a thematic "turn" between lines eight and nine, where there should be a shift in thought or perspective. The rest is up to the writer.

William Shakespeare is the best-known writer of sonnets in English, though the form originated in Renaissance Italy. Most sonnets in this book are Shakespearean in form and adhere to the same meter, rhyme scheme, and structure that he used: iambic pentameter, an ABAB/CDCD/EFEF/GG rhyme scheme, and structured as three quatrains followed by a couplet.

So what does that mean? Pentameter means there are five metric feet (main pulses) in every line, and iambs are metric feet that consist of one unaccented syllable followed by one accented syllable (ba-DUM), as in Shakespeare's "Sonnet XVIII":

Feet:	1	2	3	4	5
Pulses:	(ba-DUM)	(ba-DUM)	(ba-DUM)	(ba-DUM)	(ba-DUM)
Words:	Shall **I**	com-**pare**	thee **to**	a **sum** -	mer's **day?**

Quatrains are simply stanzas of four lines, and a couplet is a pair of lines with matching end rhymes. Shakespeare's rhyme scheme dictates that every line of a quatrain rhymes with one other line, like so:

1st Quatrain

A   Shall I compare thee to a summer's day?
B   Thou art more lovely and more temperate:
A   Rough winds do shake the darling buds of May,
B   And summer's lease hath all too short a date:

2nd Quatrain

C   Sometime too hot the eye of heaven shines,
D   And often is his gold complexion dimm'd;
C   And every fair from fair sometime declines,
D   By chance, or nature's changing course, untrimm'd;

3rd Quatrain

E   But thy eternal summer shall not fade
F   Nor lose possession of that fair thou ow'st;
E   Nor shall Death brag thou wander'st in his shade,
F   When in eternal lines to time thou grow'st;

Couplet

G   So long as men can breathe or eyes can see,
G   So long lives this, and this gives life to thee.

    The final element of the sonnet, the turn between lines eight and nine can be seen in "Sonnet XVIII" with Shakespeare's triumphant return to directly addressing his beloved, "But thy eternal summer shall not fade," and thematically there is a shift from describing that which is changeable and cyclical to that which is eternal.

    My favorite element of Shakespeare's sonnets isn't so much their form, but rather their style. I adore riding Shakespeare's train of thought through each sonnet and admire the fluidity and grace with which he states an idea in the first quatrain, develops it in the second, flips it around in the third, and caps it all off with something special in the couplet. That, far more than the meter and rhyme, is the aspect of his sonnets that I most wanted to emulate.

There are, of course, other styles of sonnets represented here. Italian sonnets in the style of Petrarch are written in two chunks, the first comprised of eight lines (the octave), and the second of six lines (the sestet), and are far more restrictively rhymed (e.g., ABBAABBA/CDCDCD). One famous example of an Italian sonnet written in English is Emma Lazarus's poem that adorns the Statue of Liberty, "The New Colossus":

Octave

A	Not like the brazen giant of Greek fame,
B	With conquering limbs astride from land to land;
B	Here at our sea-washed, sunset gates shall stand
A	A mighty woman with a torch, whose flame
A	Is the imprisoned lightning, and her name
B	Mother of Exiles. From her beacon-hand
B	Glows world-wide welcome; her mild eyes command
A	The air-bridged harbor that twin cities frame.

Sestet

C	"Keep, ancient lands, your storied pomp!" cries she
D	With silent lips. "Give me your tired, your poor,
C	Your huddled masses yearning to breathe free,
D	The wretched refuse of your teeming shore.
C	Send these, the homeless, tempest-tost to me,
D	I lift my lamp beside the golden door!"

Brava to Emma Lazarus for making the restrictive two-rhyme-pair structure work so well in English. My lone attempt at an Italian sonnet, complete with fractured Italian ("An Italian-ish Sonnet Inspired by Austrian Music," January 18th), reminded me that there are far more rhyming words in Italian than in English and taught me that I probably shouldn't attempt any more Italian sonnets, given that the whole reason I chose the sonnet was it was a form I could feasibly write well in a single day. This is why I didn't choose to write daily sestinas or villanelles ("On Villanelles, or No Villanelles," August 27th).

Thankfully, there's middle ground between the exhausting two-rhyme-pair Italian sonnet and the comparatively loosey-goosey seven-rhyme-pair Shakespearean sonnet: the Spenserian sonnet ("So Long as Men Can Breathe," February 1st), which clocks in at a creativity-challenging but not stymieing five rhyme pairs. Here's one of Edmund Spenser's most famous, "Sonnet 75" from *Amoretti*:

1st Quatrain

A	One day I wrote her name upon the strand,
B	but came the waves and washed it a way:
A	agayne I wrote it with a second hand,
B	but came the tyde, and made my paynes his pray.

2nd Quatrain

B	Vayne man, sayd she, that doest in vaine assay,
C	a mortall thing so to immortalize,
B	for I my selve shall lyke to this decay,
C	and eek my name bee wyped out lykewize.

3rd Quatrain

C	Not so, (quod I) let baser things devize
D	to dy in dust, but you shall live by fame:
C	my verse, your vertues rare shall eternize,
D	and in the hevens wryte your glorious name,

Couplet

| E | Where whenas death shall all the world subdew, |
| E | our love shall live, and later life renew. |

Of course, there are as many styles of sonnets as there are poets, which is why I felt free to play with rhyme ("Straight A's," March 24th), meter ("Fifty Meter Freestyle," June 9th), and nonsense ("An Incoherent Whatsit," October 15th). But ultimately, early and frequent exposure to Shakespeare's sonnets won out, and I'm certainly not about to complain about that, especially when deviating from him can be so much fun ("*ucking Sonnet," August 12th).

Regardless of the style of sonnet, one thing remains consistent, and that's taking the time to think about something from more than one perspective, which is predicated by the turn between lines 8 and 9 in all sonnets. One can write a sonnet about something as ordinary as a bowl of soup ("Beautiful, Beautiful Soup!" January 22nd) or as complicated as grief ("Inner Space," November 9th) and find different truths in the deliberate act of considering what something means to you at a particular moment in time. Casting about inside a day's memories for a noteworthy, beautiful, funny, or deeply-felt thought and working through it in a methodical way is as much an act of meditation as it is an act of creation.

We are fortunate to live at a time when words, definitions, synonyms, rhymes, and inspiration can be found with a few keystrokes, so the barrier to writing rhyming verse has never been lower. If this book inspires you to try your hand at writing a sonnet, and I hope it will for good ("Do You Want to Write a Sonnet?" August 28th) or ill ("A Bee in One's Sonnet," March 16th), at the very least you'll have a sonnet. But if you give yourself wholeheartedly to the enterprise, when you finish you'll have an artifact of who you were and what you thought in a specific moment of your life, an artifact that could potentially last *as long as men can breathe or eyes can see.* Or at least as long as the internet exists ("Eighteen and Up," January 20th).

January

Sonnet 101[1]

January 1st

An English sonnet's only fourteen lines,
Possessing ten and sixty metered feet,
Two stanzas of a thought, then by design,
The turn, *la volta*, where ideas meet.
The third quatrain is a kaleidoscope,
Through which the prior stanzas can be viewed.
And then a couplet which, the writer hopes,
Will emphasize or contradict the mood.
This simple form that fashion left behind
Is rarely used by poets of today,
Yet Shakespeare, Spenser, Petrarch and their kind,
While read and loved, will never fade away.
This New Year's Day has faded into night.
One down, three hundred sixty-four to write.

---

1. Punning on "101" to simultaneously suggest the course code of an introductory class and naming convention of classic sonnet cycles, to which I almost never adhered. I like that on my first day I made a thesis. "This is what a sonnet is, and this is what I'm going to do." And I did. Mostly.

New Annotated Sherlock Holmes[1] Sonnet[2]

January 2nd

While Camden House[3] lay vacant, dark, and bare,
Its counterpart on Baker Street[4] was, too.
The hunted tempted hunter to the snare,[5]
A trap was sprung, the predator subdued.[6]
An empty house, as any empty space,
Is filled with air and possibility;
Potential anything in any place,
Abounding with ineffability.
An empty hearse arrived here at my door,[7]
And hesitantly did I peer inside
Afraid of what exactly lay in store,
If I should choose to join it for a ride.
Within, I found an entertaining fiction,[8]
Which is itself a mark[9] of benediction.[10]

---

1. Title and annotations inspired by Leslie S. Klinger's *The New Annotated Sherlock Holmes* (2004). In this early sonnet, ambitious concepts and/or layered literary references overwhelm. Unless you've also been obsessed with Sherlock Holmes since you were eleven, in which case this is absolutely the sonnet for you.
2. This sonnet is my reaction to "The Empty Hearse," the first episode of the third series of the BBC television show *Sherlock*.
3. Camden House is the titular dwelling of Arthur Conan Doyle's 1903 short story "The Adventure of the Empty House," in which Sherlock Holmes was resurrected after his "death" at Reichenbach Falls.
4. Opposite Camden House is 221b Baker Street, the flat that Sherlock Holmes and Doctor Watson occupied during many of their adventures.
5. In "The Adventure of the Empty House," Sherlock Holmes revealed the existence the late Professor Moriarty's confederate, Sebastian Moran.
6. Holmes tricked Moran into attempting to assassinate him, which ensured Moran's arrest and connected him with a prior murder via his unique air gun.
7. A nod to Emily Dickinson's poem "Because I could not stop for Death."
8. The episode contains several explanations of how Sherlock could have survived his apparent suicide. Due to unreliable narrators, it's unclear which, if any, of them, is accurate. Very *Rashomon*.
9. Pun on the name of the co-creator of Sherlock, Mark Gatiss, who wrote "The Empty Hearse" and played Mycroft Holmes.
10. Pun on Benedict Cumberbatch, the actor who plays Sherlock.

Mising Leter Sonet[1]

January 3rd

As a new standup comic on the stag
Whose never-tested japeries fall fat,
And facing down the hostile masses' rag
Must tap reserves of courage in his hat[2]—
So I, when looking down this rocky rod
I took, not knowing what would lie ahad,
Must persevere, though failure bumps forebod,
And hope the hindrances won't be widesprad.
So when at night one wakens from one's slee
To find in mind poor Wordsworth's lonely clod[3]
The joke may be considered somewhat chea
But precious if it makes one laugh alod.
Instead of feeling funerals in my brin[4]
Some silly found me worthy and did dign.[5]

---

1. The first of many silly sonnets, this one removes one or more letters from the last word of every line. I made actual words in the first stanza but decided it was easier (and possibly funnier) to use nonsense words after that.
2. Plays with William Shakespeare's "Sonnet XXIII."
3. Refers to William Wordsworth's poem "I wandered lonely as a cloud."
4. Plays with Emily Dickinson's poem "I felt a Funeral, in my Brain." I wanted to include "I felt a funeral in my bran" but couldn't fit it in, alas.
5. Refers to Sidney Royse Lysaght's poem "Penalty of Love."

Sonnet for Giovanni[1]

January 4th

Familiaris[2] as could ever be,
A hundred thousand years from *lupus* split,
Beloved *canis*, lying on my knee,
Whenever in my domicile I sit.
Your wee black nose, more sensitive than mine
A millionfold, and dichromatic vision,
Developed for the hunt, these days malign
Most frequently to butter, steak, and pigeon.
I know that the behaviors I adore
Are products of our long co-evolution,
Inherited from social carnivores,
To whom you seem a scruffy Lilliputian.
And yet, I know I couldn't ever choose
If asked to say whose nature nurtured whose.

---

1. The first of many sonnets about my dogs, Giovanni the terrier mix and Hildegard the Überdachshund. This one was inspired by the character of Data from *Star Trek: The Next Generation*, who wrote a highly scientific ode to his cat Spot in the episode "Schisms."
2. The adorable scientific name for the domestic dog is *Canis lupus familiaris*.

Onomatopoeia Sonnet[1]

January 5th

Drone. Ribbit. Humm. Snap! Whuff? Sniff. Shuffle. Howl!
Crunch-Crunch-Crunch. Thud! Crash! Rustle! Dash-Dash-Dash!
Pant-Pant. Susurrus. Swallow. Silence. Growl.
Crunch-Crack! Snag-Rustle! Squelch-squelch! Hurk! Ker-SPLASH!
Slosh-sloshing; murmur, hissing. Gurgle-thump!!
Gasp! Dripping dribble! Moan. *Ka-CHUNK! Ker-BLAM!*
Whizz! Tchick! UH! Groan! Sprint-sprint-sprint! Snag! Ergh! Bump!
AIEEEE! Scrunch! Cough! Gasp! Rasping. Wince. Urgh. Slam!——
Clasp. Hoist. Ugh! Squishing. Gasping. *Whew!* Honk honk!
Grunt. Scraping limp. Thump! Slam! Rasp gasp! Pause. SMACK!
OW! Growl, groan, wrestle! Sniff. Snort. Giggle. Bonk.
Smooch, moaning, nipping. Tap. *Ka-CHUNK! Crack! Crack!*
Crash! Tinkle! DUCK! Brace! Rumble. Tic. *Ka-BOOM!*
Grasp. Chuckle. Smooch. Click. Roar. Shift. Squeal. Va-ROOM!

---

1. In this sonnet, I attempted to tell a James Bond-type action tale in onomatopoeia, and it didn't entirely work on several levels, the most basic of which is that not all syllables used are actually onomatopoeia. On the bright side, the act of failing to match my output to my vision so early in the project was a valuable lesson on letting go when an idea isn't working. It was also a sign that attempting restrictive, high-concept sonnets might not result in my best work.

On Public Transportation[1]

January 6th

Sometimes, when buying groceries in a store,
And, after waiting patiently in line,
One customer between me and the door,
A register will open next to mine.
Annoyance sprung from that pales in compare
To helplessly observe across the street
The bus, on which you are a frequent fare,
Depart, its tail-lights flashing your defeat.
And yet, when to that frigid[2] bench I sink,
Disgruntled, chilled, and more than slightly vexed,
I find that when I seize the time to think,
It helps me focus on whatever's next.
The next time inconvenience makes me miffed,
I'll try to see forced stillness as a gift.

---

1. Not coincidentally, this was the first sonnet written entirely on my morning commute.
2. Frigid by southern California standards, anyway. It was 40° Fahrenheit!

7

Cornelius[1]

January 7th

As energy within covalent bonds,
Electrons joyful in an orbit shared,
Until reaction forces them beyond
Their current state, released into the air—
Thus, love between two beings, when at rest,
Gives comfort to the pair who share the tie.
In giving self, each partner is twice-blessed,
For even when the time is right to die,
That sudden separation brings great pain,
And yet, it issues to the universe
A measure of immeasurable gain,
And none of us can ever be the worse.
While love will be inevitably severed,
Embracing it, we change the world forever.

---

1. *In memoriam* my friend Susanna's beloved cat. These thoughts about death were partially inspired by "Ineffable", from David Eagleman's book *Sum: Tales from the Afterlives,* which I heard on *Radiolab* in 2012 a week after a friend passed away unexpectedly at the age of 35 (see "Summarizing Proust," June 10th and "Nota Bene," November 17th).

Marine Layer[1]

January 8th

Outside my bedroom window was a blank;
Familiar hidden by a fallen cloud—
In its embrace all noise and sunlight sank,
To sleep beneath the insubstantial shroud.
I yearned to run outside and gladly fill
My lungs with cool, rejuvenating haze,
To breathe the silence and the morning chill,
To pull my mind from its lethargic daze.
But no; when I stepped forth to meet the day,
I found no fog, just shining, dewy turf.
The morning's blanket had been tucked away
Between horizon and the distant surf.
And though the sun forced morning to unveil,
I made my own mist each time I exhaled.

---

1. Marine layer is a mass of air that forms over a body of water that frequently results in low-altitude stratus clouds, also known as sea fog (though not actually fog). In San Diego, marine layer frequently rolls in from the ocean in the evenings and can linger through mid-morning.

The Prince[1]

January 9th

From squalid soil a shriveled sapling sprang,
Which grew into a convoluted tree,
Whose listless leaves from blackened branches hang,
And twisted shape compels the birds to flee.
It gives no shade or succor to the tired,
And bears no fruits or flowers on its limbs.
Abhorrence and disquiet it inspires,
Except in those who offer it a hymn.
For though the tree fell many seasons past,
In falling, it revealed its fortitude,
For fire, disease, and drought did it outlast,
And by its loss, the forest was renewed.
And in the spring, when sunshine melts the snows,
Within its limbs, a silver lily[2] grows.

---

1. Refers to "Half-Blood Prince," the nickname of Severus Snape in J. K. Rowling's *Harry Potter* series. His birthday is January 9th.
2. A reference to Lily Potter, Snape's childhood friend and unrequited crush, also the mother of Harry Potter. Oh yeah. Spoilers?

Calypte anna[1]

January 10th

Whilst wandering between my workday tasks,
I paused upon a pavement near a tree,
And squinted through its leaves as if to ask
Just who it was that chittered thus at me.
And perched upon the loftiest of twigs
A hummingbird, afluff in coat of green,
Magenta scarf, and iridescent wig,
Demanded the location of his queen.
Delighted, how I wished I could preserve
His earnest likeness in my phone, but no,
It lay upon my desk; so I observed
A moment between him and me alone.
His tirade and conspicuous array,
In memory I'll frequently replay.

---

1. The scientific name for Anna's hummingbird, a common species on the Pacific Coast.
They're beautiful, with iridescent green and fuchsia feathers, and like other hummingbird
species, noisy and delightfully ill-tempered.

A Sonnet by Hildegard, Überdachshund[1]

January 11th

As I survey my kingdom, grass and trees,
My eyes are keen to catch the slightest twitch,
My nose is primed for odors on the breeze
Like me, the Feline Menace[2] is a bitch.
For when our borders daily I patrol,
And I flush out the hissing, fluffy foe,
The Idiots in Charge[3] think it's a stroll,
And though I yank, they never let me go.
When empty-pawed I come home from the hunt,
The Idiots assuage my pain with treats,
Such paltry offerings are an affront,
And yet, my stomach orders me to eat.
And though with feline presence I'm obtruded,
I find small comfort, still, in being fooded.

---

1. Hildy really is the largest dachshund I've ever seen. And like all dachshunds, she's
convinced she's even bigger than she actually is.
2. The most familiar members of the Feline Menace are our neighbors' outdoor cats,
particularly marmalade tom Oliver and tuxedo Joey, who pal around in front of our house.
3. She is unconvinced that I have reliable ways of detecting danger or determining threats.

An Unlucky Charge[1]

January 12th

A playoff loss has brought our season's end,
And while it would have been a joy to see
Not just one quarter's worth of scoring trend,
And penalties and sacks the other three——
The onside kick was thrilling, our success
Rejuvenated fan and team morale.
The turnaround caused Denverites distress,
Was Mile High now a lucky Bolts locale?
Alas, when Bronco offense took the field,
Our defense did their running game transcend,
So to the clock the Chargers had to yield,
One touchdown short of overtime. The end.
And yet, who out there doesn't want to see
Continued Brady-Manning[2] rivalry?

---

1. A pun on San Diego's (now former) professional football team, the Chargers (aka the Bolts), alluding to their post-season loss to the Denver Broncos, whose home field is in Mile High Stadium.
2. Long-standing friendly rivalry between two great quarterbacks, Tom Brady of the New England Patriots and Peyton Manning of the Denver Broncos (formerly of the Indianapolis Colts).

Reflections[1]

January 13th

While on unbroken paths today I roved,
Persuaded by a minor injury,[2]
I found myself within a sunny grove,
Whose eucalyptus contemplated me.
I paused to meet one's eye, and there I found
That to the trunk small mirrors had been fixed,
The joints and knots now winked, and all around
Reflection, art, and fancy intermixed.
And later, from behind a mirrored wall[3]
I sat, observing people stop and stare,
Not seeing me, succumbing to the thrall,
Of their own visages reflected there.
I wondered as I smiled and watched them preen,
When I stopped by the trees, who might have seen?

---

1. Inspired by Keenan Harsten's art installation entitled *Naught* (2010), which was a site-specific "intervention" intended to cause a shift of awareness in the viewer. The artist affixed small mirrors to knots on eucalyptus trees in the center of UC San Diego's campus. A video about this project may be seen at http://vimeo.com/16218659 .
2. Mild shin splints, which made walking on soft surfaces preferable to paved.
3. A dining area in the student center.

Life Lessons 3,284,925 to 3,284,934[1]

January 14th

Keep dogs away from bushes on your walks,
For food and varmints draw them by the nose.
With rubber boots, eschew short cotton socks
Unless you like them crumpled 'twixt your toes.
When eating ramen, cool it as you slurp.
Gel pads in old brassieres can spring a leak.
Horchata plus prosecco makes a burp
That past piña coladas does bespeak.
A sled is not a surfboard—you can't steer.
Machines work better when you turn them on.
You catch more flies with cognac than with beer.
And smiling for a camera makes you yawn.
Such lessons may not be much fun to learn,
But laughter at recounting them's well-earned.

---

1. I don't actually number every lesson I learn through experience, but I suspect I've had at least this many. Continued in "More Life Lessons," May 20th.

A Soonerism Sponnet[1]

January 15th

When due to lengthy days my grain brows tired
My langurative figuage can get skewed,
As if my cerebellum is woss-crired,
Producing oddities that round quite sude.
These stunning cunts of speech make consequent
That I am comprecult to diffihend.
When only I can tell just mutt is whent,
I'm tempted to let dilences sescend.
But on such days when my toor pongue is tied,
Frustration to the weastern ind I fling,
I brake a teath and cease myself to chide,
Remembering, "Don't pet the sweaty things."[2]
When spibberish I gout, patience I plea,
I lake mess sense when I speak normally.

---

1. A Spoonerism occurs when a speaker switches the initial sounds of two words, such as saying "The Lord is a shoving leopard" instead of "The Lord is a loving shepherd." Spoonerisms are named for William Archibald Spooner, who made at least one of them within earshot of his students at Oxford. Few of the many others attributed to him have been substantiated, says language and humor wonk Richard Lederer. They are, however, still funny.
2. A great Spoonerism from George Carlin: "Don't sweat the petty things, and don't pet the sweaty things."

16

Meh[1]

January 16th

I do not wish to write a poem today.
I'm tired and do not have an ounce of wit.
I can't think of a blessed thing to say,
And if I did, it likely wouldn't fit
In fourteen lines; my thoughts could be so small,
They'd barely fill a stanza, or they might
Require a sonnet cycle for them all,
Thus keeping me from sleep another night.
And as I lay awake that sleepless night,
I'd curse wrong-sized ideas that grow like weeds,
For though they may entice with colors bright,
They're best ripped out before they go to seed.
This is a quite discursive way to say,
That I don't wish to write a poem today.

---

1. This sonnet is a bit of an oxymoron, because the reason I didn't wish to write a poem was that I didn't like any of the ideas I'd had. Of course, then I realized that "I do not wish to write a poem today" is a pretty good first line. And once I had a subject and a first line, I was off and running with my anxieties about ideas that were too big or complicated to force into a tolerable sonnet in a day. I did get better at this as time went on.

Consummation[1]

January 17th

I think I have been drunk too much this week,
Consuming all and being thus consumed.
And though this madness on myself I wreaked,
The mania is heady as perfume.
Across the world the feverish unite,
Awash in anxious hopes and nameless fears,
Prepared to praise and curse the very sight
Of episodes for which we've waited years.
The time for moderation will return,
And with it my responsibilities.
I'll sweep the ashes of our passion burned,
And lock the fire away with practiced ease.
For being drunk's no thing to sugar-coat:
Just ask a glass of water, Adams wrote.[2]

---

1. As Mae West said, "Too much of a good thing is great." And this is what happens when
Sherlock fans, who had been waiting for years for new episodes, suddenly had three new ones
to enjoy.
2. A joke from Douglas Adams's *The Hitchhiker's Guide to the Galaxy*.

An Italian-ish[1] Sonnet[2] Inspired by Austrian Music

January 18th

I breakfasted with Mozart Saturday:
Fantasia on *"Là ci darem la mano,"*[3]
For clarinet, not baritone/soprano,
So gone was the seductive interplay
Between the ingenue, whose fiancé
Would disapprove, and Count, whose *andiamo*[4]
Is more than just a dance, *comprendiamo,*[5]
The dainty steps of being led astray.
But seated also here, my own Masetto[6]
Engrossed in lesson planning, the curator
Of variations, partners my duet,
And thusly knows the words. *Mi cor, affretto*[7]
Take one *bacetto,*[8] and my vow that later
I'll make you glad you married the coquette.

---

1. My Italian is not what it once was. Or perhaps never was.
2. My lone attempt an Italian/Petrarchian sonnet, which has a stricter rhyme scheme and a two-part structure, compared with the four stanzas followed by a couplet of Shakespearean sonnets.
3. A lovely duet from *Don Giovanni* between the titular nobleman and the flirtatious peasant girl Zerlina.
4. "Come hither."
5. "I get it."
6. Masetto is Zerlina's long-suffering fiancé, whom she marries despite Don Giovanni's best efforts.
7. This was supposed to mean, "My heart, make haste."
8. Smooch.

What Dreams May Come[1]

January 19th

I closed a book of poems[2] and my eyes,
And as I drifted softly into sleep,
A voice inside my mind began to rise
Mellifluous enough to make one weep.
I can't recall exactly what it said,
If Shelley, Blake, or Keats, I couldn't say.
My body froze abruptly, full of dread,
Anticipating what I might betray
At such a feast of supple sibilants,
A plethora of lustrous labiodentals,
Melodious vowels, the sort of sound that haunts
Musicians' minds; vibrations transcendental.
And though I lost the words, the voice remains
Its gentle rhythm pulsing in my veins.

1. From Hamlet's famous "To be or not to be..." speech in act 3, scene 1 of Shakespeare's *Hamlet*.
2. I was poking about in my *Norton Anthology of English Literature* before bedtime. It was actually Keats.

Eighteen and Up[1]

January 20th

Each moment has a truth that can be caught,
In picture, memory, or written word,
So even when the context is forgot,
The meaning may be someday disinterred.
And even though I lived too late to see
Just who was darling as the buds of May,
That is the least important part to me;
What lingers is what Shakespeare felt that day.
And yet, before you share your truth, take heed:
All things leave traces in this day and age.
Like Frankenstein, someday your heart may bleed
For what you left in hubris, fear, or rage.
As long as engines search and chats roulette,
Your truth has life upon the internet.

---

1. Punning on age-restricted content and Shakespeare's "Sonnet XVIII" ("Shall I compare
thee to a Summer's day.").

Unexpected Kindnesses

January 21st

This morning of discomfort seemed a test
Compounded by a dreadful weariness,
A list of tasks to daunt the doughtiest,
And not a moment's peace to convalesce.
Impediments aplenty multiplied,
The burning candle's ends should then have met,
And when my desperation I implied,
A Montague beseeched a Capulet.[1]
But help arrived in stranger's kindly act;
A sad goodbye turned into bye-for-now,
It was the box, not me that substance lacked,[2]
My gratitude for this I will avow:
That when I reach the end, I dare to hope,
That always there will be another rope.

---

1. Refers to the feuding families in Shakespeare's *Romeo and Juliet*.
2. A structural failure was deemed to have been caused by forces beyond my control.

Beautiful, Beautiful Soup![1]

January 22nd

A steaming robin's egg with noodles filled,
With scallion green and ginger red bedecked,
And brown with brine, a treasure chest that spilled
Its gold into a sea with flotsam flecked.
Above, the humble offering of pork
Enriches all the contents of the bowl.
One dare not denigrate it with a fork;
But gently nibbled, it will warm the soul.
I navigate the depths with sticks and spoon
Withdrawing golden tresses from within
And sipping them, I cannot help but croon,
Intense umami, yet as smooth as sin.
A sacrament to Pastafarians:[2]
To that, I'll raise my voice in sweet rAmens.

---

1. From Lewis Carroll's poem "Beautiful Soup." A sonnet in praise of ramen, upon which I relied heavily during my sonnet writing for physical and arguably spiritual nourishment.
2. A reference to the Church of the Flying Spaghetti Monster, a satirical fellowship intended to illustrate the absurdity of the state endorsing religious doctrine. "rAmen!" is one of their punny exclamations.

Be Happy[1]

January 23rd

"Be happy!" said the parking lot. I was;
My lowered gaze, I thought, was not produced
By sadness, yet the painted words gave pause;
Had my own happiness become diffuse?
My first reaction was to laugh and scoff,
Because to optimism I'm inclined,
Yet thinking on the day, its crests and troughs,
The disappointments lingered in my mind.
But that poor lot, oppressed by countless tires,
Still had its cheerful wisdom to dispense
In crudely painted letters; the desire
To give good cheer to those who wandered hence.
If it can smile despite the trash and shit
Perhaps there's something to be learned from it.

---

1. Another sonnet based on a chance encounter, in this case, with a graffito spray painted on the asphalt of a nearby parking lot. There was also a smiley face.

24

A Toast[1]

January 24th

The rules insist that when you drop your toast,
It lands with jelly side against the ground,
Unless, the cynic offers as riposte,
Through luck, it lands the other way around—
Because the inconvenience and the mess,
Delay the meal as one cleans off the rug,
Those vexing memories the mind impress;
Good fortune is forgotten with a shrug.
Exceptions frequently disprove the rule,
Yet we prefer the patterns of the bad,
So never let me be the kind of fool
Who misses all the things that make one glad.
But on some days, the good leaves one nonplussed,
Like when the dropped toast lands upon its crust.

---

1. I'm all for metaphor, but if you drop a piece of toast that lands perfectly balanced on its crust, you write about it.

On Working Mendelssohn's *Lobgesang*[1]

January 25th

When working on a project of some length
We are advised to learn it bit by bit,
To gently test endurance and one's strength,
While living with the fear one might omit
A necessary passage or to find
That when a crucial section is rehearsed,
You realize that you are flying blind,[i]
And panic renders reading even worse.
And thus, when your director says, "Let's run
The piece straight through and see what needs some work,"
Then suddenly, rehearsal turns to fun,
Which feeds a new resolve to never shirk.
So when we sing *vergangen ist die Nacht*,[2]
It feels as though *gekommen ist der Tag*.[3]

---

1. Felix Mendelssohn's 1840 Symphony no. 2 in B-flat minor, op. 52, for chorus, orchestra and soloists. This "hymn of praise" was composed to celebrate the 400th anniversary of the invention of the printing press, which led to the democratization of learning. There's a lot of light-of-knowledge/dark-of-ignorance imagery in the text.
2. "The night has passed."
3. "The day has come." Mendelssohn wasn't too fussed by the dearth of perfect end rhymes in the text he set, so I felt justified in using assonance here.

There's the Rub[1]

January 26th

What one can do on any given day
Sometimes amazes when reflected on,
But other times it brings profound dismay
To think of all the tasks one left undone.
Such days can lead to restless, fitful nights
In which the mind can't be dissuaded from
Revisiting one's slips and oversights;
Obsessively accounting what's to come
Until exhaustion settles on the brain,
And smothers all the nagging voices, yet
The ghosts of castigation will remain:
Disturbing dreams that one cannot forget.
Ironic that these worrying mistakes
Are the result of being kept awake.

---

1. Another reference to Hamlet's "To be or not to be" speech from *Hamlet,* act 3, scene.

TAS (The Acronym Sonnet)

January 27th

There must be something in our DNA
Or in our language roots or ABCs,
That makes us love our shortcuts. MLA[1]
Provides just one of many SOPs:[2]
You needn't spell out acronyms like RADAR—
Like SCUBA, it's in fairly frequent use.
Pronounce as words such entities as SPAWAR,[3]
To find their meanings, check their FAQs.
With chatting slang, just shrug and LOL
Or say that you were just now AFK;[4]
You're only ever truly SOL[5]
When lacking context equals IDK.[6]
And while such things will work for A/S/L,[7]
ILU[8] is much better IRL.[9]

---

1. Modern Language Association.
2. Standard Operating Procedures.
3. Space and Naval Warfare Systems Command. More like an abbreviation than an acronym, but it was the only thing I could come up with that rhymed with RADAR.
4. Away From the Keyboard.
5. Shit Out of Luck.
6. I Don't Know.
7. Age/Sex/Location, common introductory question in internet chat.
8. I Love You. And I do if you are reading this footnote. XOXOXOX
9. In Real Life.

To Kazoos[1]

January 28th

From ritual and dance that strove to hide
Identities from watchers' ears and eyes,
Descended the kazoo, for years supplied
By parents in response to children's cries.
But when that cheerful buzzing banishes
The woeful din, it substitutes a sound
At which all satisfaction vanishes;
Faust would admit the quandary profound.
But kitschy and obnoxious though it seems,
Its own diminished form it can transcend;
In concert context it is gaining steam,
Within a playful and nostalgic trend.
To thoughtful artists, it presents the choice
Of just how silly one should make one's voice.

---

1. In celebration of National Kazoo Day, which the UC San Diego Arts Library celebrates
with a concert organized by Scott Paulson, which features commissioned works for kazoo.

Sightedness[1]

January 29th

When one's world starts to lose its clarity,
Corrective lenses often are assigned
So one perceives the world in verity,
Each leaf and pixel perfectly defined.
Alas, there are no spectacles for minds,
Nor any remedy for wayward thoughts
Through medication some their focus find,
And meditation can be learned and taught.
But when one chooses to remove the specs,
The world is filled with wonders, every light
Becomes a geometric form complex,
Like dandelions at seed in colors bright.
Distorted vision sometimes helps one see
The things that are as they're supposed to be.

---

1. When riding back to San Diego after a Los Angeles Philharmonic concert, I removed my glasses to rub my eyes, and when I took my hands away, I discovered that my brain was filling in illusive geometric patterns in the blurry freeway lights, headlights, and taillights. It was strange and beautiful and something I've enjoyed repeating under similar circumstances. It's one of the few advantages of having terrible vision.

Concerning Limericks[1]

January 30th

While sonnets have their devotees, too few
Respect the limerick as poetry,
While citing violations of taboo,
As if perdition came from childish glee.
Transgression, true, is in the poem's soul,
To laugh at human idiosyncrasy,
And mock the powers seeking to control
Behavior and enforce morality.
And yet, when I take up my pen to write,
I can't escape those lettered luminaries
Whose limericks both gladden and delight;
Sublimely silly, revolutionary.
Like Lear[2] and Stoppard,[3] see a trend and buck it,
Just like that cheeky fellow from Nantucket.[4]

---

1. As seen in "To Kazoos" (January 28th), I find it fun to write sonnets about less rarefied subjects than love and death.
2. Edward Lear, a great writer of limericks and other nonsense verse.
3. Tom Stoppard wrote an entire scene in limericks in his play *Travesties.*
4. Though many exceptionally rude limericks begin with "There once was a man from Nantucket," the first recorded examples were puns on New England place names. *There once was a man from Nantucket/Who kept all his cash in a bucket./His daughter named Nan/Ran off with a man/And as for the bucket, Nantucket.*

Concerning Clerihews[1]

January 31st

A clever man was Edmund Clerihew
Bentley; a novelist, comedic gem,
And counted thus among the very few
Who have a type of poem named for them.
It started as a sort of schoolboy lark
To help recall a chemist's famous deed,[2]
And with that salty rhyme he made his mark,
And scribes like Auden[3] followed Bentley's lead.
While tortured meter and a sense of fun
Make silly verses pointless to impeach,
Their aim is not just satire or to pun,
But rather fundamentally to teach.
So thank the clerihew if you recall
The architect who realized St. Paul's.[4]

---

1. Clerihews are four-line biographical poems with humorously appalling rhyme and meter.
2. Sir Humphrey Davy/Abominated gravy./He lived in the odium/Of having discovered sodium. (E. C. Bentley)
3. When the young Kant/Was told to kiss his aunt,/He obeyed the Categorical Must,/But only just. (W. H. Auden)
4. Christopher Wren/Said, "I am going to dine with some men,/If anyone calls,/Say I am designing St. Paul's." (E. C. Bentley)

February

So Long as Men Can Breathe[1]

February 1st

To read a sonnet written to a love
Means learning nothing of that paramour,
We know the poet might have got her glove,
But of her character we'll know no more.
Who did she love? With whom had she rapport?
What did she want of life? What were her dreams?
Enduring fame from poet guarantor
Is not the splendid tribute that it seems.
"I deeply loved!" is poet's chosen theme,
And that's the sentiment that's given life
And by a certain reader type esteemed—
Those less concerned with loving than with strife.
So, thanks for offered immortality;
I'd rather what I did give life to me.

---

1. Another response to Shakespeare's "Sonnet XVIII" (see "Eighteen and Up," January 20th). Also inspired by similar themes in Spenser's "Amoretti: Sonnet LXXV" and Sir Walter Raleigh's "The Nymph's Response to the Shepherd."

The SuperB Owl[1]

February 2nd

A superb owl alighted next to me,
With plumage bright and captivating call,
Its annual visit easy to foresee,
As was the promise we should have a ball.
And while its blandishments were a temptation,
I noticed that its wings were all askew,
So rather than great feats of aviation,
A lot of feckless fluttering ensued.
Though there was satisfaction to be found
By those who like to cheer for gravity,
The contest never quite got off the ground,
And far less fun for lack of equity.
Repeated disappointment can't belie
The fable that the superb owl can fly.

---

1. A pun on Super Bowl stolen shamelessly from Wil Wheaton, which functions here as an extended metaphor for Super Bowl XLVIII, which was a lopsided victory by the Seattle Seahawks over the Denver Broncos.

Good Night Sweet Prince[1]

February 3rd

An actor dies in New York every day
And leaves no more or less than any man;
Remembered for the roles he once portrayed
By colleagues, family, and ardent fans.
An actor died in New York yesterday,[2]
Who with his presence stage and film had graced,
And while we mourn his loss, we yet betray
An underlying sentiment of waste.
The shadows swallowed yet another light,
And for its lack, the firmament is dimmed.
He walked a long day's journey into night,[3]
The undertaking proved too much for him.
Within addiction's greater tragedy,
His passing marks the climax of Act III.[4]

---

1. From *Hamlet,* act 5, scene 2.
2. *In memoriam* Philip Seymour Hoffman, 1967-2014.
3. Refers to Eugene O'Neill's play *Long Day's Journey Into Night,* which deals with addiction in many forms, the malady that led to Hoffman's passing.
4. Optimistic hope that because Hoffman was open about his struggles with addiction, and because of his support of others who struggled to remain sober, his passing may erase some of the stigma that prevents so many from seeking help.

Distractingly Attractive[1]

February 4th

My days are often drenched with pulchritude,
And though I'm grateful for its copiousness,
Some situations beg me to conclude
There's such a thing as beauty to excess.
On handsome men I usually bestow
A smile or cheerful greeting, but there's one
Whose glorious perfection brings me woe
Because his presence interrupts my tongue.
An aspect of his fineness undefined
Short-circuits my attempts at fluency,
My word retrieval slackens to a grind,
And awkwardness derails my raillery.[2]
Abandoned by linguistic competence,
A smile and wave may be my best defense.

---

1. It can be difficult to regularly interact someone you find so attractive that you're unable to speak coherently. Entertaining, though.
2. My conversation was once so awkward that he stopped and pretended to tie his shoe so he wouldn't have to keep walking with me. Honestly, I was more relieved than embarrassed.

Murphy's Law[1] of Choral Masterworks[2]

February 5th

The first time Maestro runs us through the score
There rises an impending sense of dread
As details we've rehearsed go out the door,
And what we've practiced ends up on its head.
Pronunciations and dynamics shift;
We drill refinements 'til our minds are numb.
Our pencils fly, lest we be left adrift,
Our folders bursting with eraser crumbs.
But when the orchestra begins to play,
And soloists make movements seem a whole
Fastidiousness is thoroughly repaid,
And moments of transcendence feed the soul.
But our improvement's due for a reversal
About the time we have our dress rehearsal.

---

1. Shorthand for "if something can go wrong, it will." Also known as Sod's Law.
2. San Diego Master Chorale (including me) sang Mendelssohn's *Lobgesang* with the San Diego Symphony Orchestra.

A Sonnet by Giovanni, a Dog Who May Be Part Cat[1]

February 6th

Obtaining sustenance is such a chore
That there are days I lack the will to try.
For why should I have kibble on the floor
When lovely odors drift down from on high?
And when I leap to that ambrosial place
My inborn grace receives no word of praise.
I'm shooed away, my bowl shoved in my face,
While fixed in an unblinking, baleful gaze.
But when I deign to nose my meager meal,
I jump, when in the corner of my eye
A sudden movement! I spin on my heel,
And find my tail. It's hard to recognize!
And if there's nothing better I could do
I might consent to take a bite or two.

---

1. It is one of the household theories that our terrier mix Giovanni is part cat because he snubs his food (unless it is cheese), frequently leaps up to places he is not allowed, and is often surprised by his own tail, hence this sonnet from his perspective. One of the other prevailing theories, based solely on appearance, is that he is a toy wolfhound.

Little Bits[1]

A run-through is a satisfying thing:
To hear where your part fits within the whole,
And learn the proper place to stand and sing,
And feel as though all share common goal.
But when the final notes have dissipated,
There's hardly time to celebrate success;
Our egos will be presently deflated,
As little bits of music we address.
A little bit less here, and don't crescendo!
A little bit connected: *non marcato*!
A little bit less there, diminuendo!
A little bit more accent—it's staccato!
A little bit disheartening it may be,
But in the details one finds artistry.

---

1. Inspired by a charming verbal tic of a frequent musical collaborator, which is the repeated use of "little bit" to describe requested changes, as shown in the third stanza. Singers have been known to keep count of the number of times "little bit" is uttered and compare totals at the end of rehearsal.

Uniformity[1]

February 8th

In any group that wears a uniform,
A number of disparities you'll see,
As some are souls who don't like to conform,
And others that transgress unwittingly.
Some men forgo the recommended vest,
And ladies' skirts don't hide their patterned hose,
And to be fair, the handbook's not expressed
A ruling on the rings in brows and nose.
But I prefer to outwardly comply,
Since who would think the lady singing psalms
Would wear black hose that come up to her thighs
And scarlet garter belt with such aplomb?
Though some find such requirements oppression
There's always room for subtle self-expression.

---

1. Many choirs have a required uniform that all singers must wear for performances. Men are often allowed to wear their own tuxedos, but the uniform outfits for women are frequently awful.

Free Time, or Lack Thereof[1]

February 9th

It's been so long since I had any time
That wasn't promised to a type of work,
At first such freedom seems a thing sublime,
But then I wonder if I haven't shirked
Some task that I've forgotten—it's as though
My brain is so accustomed to the load,
That when it goes from overwhelmed to slow,
It lacks the skill to totally unload.
Instead of viral videos and memes,
To pass the time, I might just read a book.
Or write a fugue, or join a rugby team,
Or organize the perfect writing nook.
So may these precious, unexpected hours
Encourage postponed daydreams into flower.

---

1. Written after our third and final performance of Mendelssohn's "Lobgesang." It's incredibly satisfying to perform music one has rehearsed for months and with great intensity and to perform it well. Alas, post-performance crash usually follows.

Bones[1]

February 10th

While navigating busy thoroughfares,
It's always a fortuitous surprise,
When someone notices that you are there
And has the confidence to meet your eyes
As if to say, "I see you are like me,
A person who is patently aware
That people hide within humanity,
But can be found by those who look with care."
Such people scatter bones along the way,
Upon injustices or penury.
By doing what they can to help today,
They alter our collective memory.
The choice to see with altruistic blindness,
Depends upon that armature of kindness.

---

1. Though one sees and is seen by many people when one rides the bus to and from work, moments of connection and recognition are rarer.

Pollen Good Time[1]

February 11th

An arching pine, bedecked with pollen cones,
Invites the birds as well as curious fingers.
Though it may make some sneeze when it is blown,
When touched, the gold corona rarely lingers.
Upon a limb a tanager alights,
From twig to twig the clever sparrows dart,
Distinctly they arrive with colors bright,
But counterfeit goldfinches they depart.
A monoecious[2] conifer that vexes
Each entity it generously dusts,
It bears the structures of two separate sexes,
So why these sordid sorties aimed at us?
Perhaps that tree and I do think as one,
Since making messes is a lot of fun.

---

1. A punning title to draw attention from the fact that this is a sonnet about tree sex.
2. A plant that has both male and female reproductive parts.

Concerning Haiku

A poem that has fourteen rhyming lines
Without a turn is not a sonnet, true,
And syllables, if carefully designed
But lack a cut,[1] do not comprise haiku.
The forms, distinct, share one important trait:
A change in tone dividing different parts.
Instead of lines that basically conflate,
Contrasting concepts fresh ideas impart.
So if you must compose haiku in jest,
Satirically extolling the banal,
Take one step back and see if you've expressed
A thought that cuts through repetition's pall.
If this requirement is too much for you,
I might suggest you try a Clerihew.[2]

---

1. The juxtaposition of two different images or ideas and revealing them to be related.
2. See "Concerning Clerihews" (January 31st).

45

A Grate Sonnet[1]

February 13th

In days of your, there lessons were quite strict,
And everybody knew witch word to use.
But nowadays yore likely to be tricked
By homophones in writing ewe peruse.
Such errors have become ubiquitous:
Its pointless to point every error out—
Your likely to be called punctilious
Or worse, to feel a moment of self-doubt.
Four when a clever friend's the one to make
The lapse, theirs consequent uncertainty;
Who's instincts are at fault for the mistake?
Who's brain misfired, albeit partially?
Retreat then, to you're trusty usage guide,
To tell the truth from lies, lay, laid, and lied.

---

1. This sonnet gleefully highlights common (and less common) errors caused by
homophones. The title both puns as a homophone for "great" and functions literally,
because such goofs grate on those who are particular about grammar and usage.

For My Valentine[1]

February 14th

The world is full of flowers for the day.
At intersections pop-up tents will sprout
And underneath the desperate can pay
For roses so their mates won't go without.
But blossoms, teddy bears, and chocolate hearts
While pleasant for a day, cannot compare
To kindnesses that set my love apart
And seem to me ubiquitous as air.
My love is lovely, yet he's so much more,
Than limbs and kisses that I do desire,
And though his russet tresses I adore,
He's admirable, beyond what I admire.
Those goodly parts of which he is comprised
Allow him yet to take me by surprise.

---

1. Part of me thinks it's a bit sad that I wrote more sonnets about my dogs than about my remarkable spouse. But that's mostly because my dogs can't read and are therefore unlikely to be embarrassed by what I write about them. However, if I can't write a romantic sonnet on Valentine's Day, when can I?

On *Coriolanus*,[1] *Bethany*,[2] and *The Elixir of Love*[3]

February 15th

On Thursday, an immortal voice was heard;
On Friday, a contemporary one,
On Saturday, an opera absurd,
But filled with gorgeous music, verve, and fun.
Three works that have completely different tones,
But even the historic tragedy
Shares story arcs, some key thematic bones,
And caustic wit with Friday's comedy.
Though you may laugh to think these disparate plays
Would share a thing with Donizetti, yet
Like Martius, Adina too betrays;
Like Crystal, Nemorino's hard to get.
Catharsis, bleakness, laughter, desperation——
I'm glad art rarely trades in moderation.

---

1. National Theatre Live's production of Shakespeare's *Coriolanus,* shown in cinemas around the world.
2. The Old Globe's production of Laura Marks's play *Bethany.*
3. San Diego Opera's production of Gaetano Donizetti's opera *The Elixir of Love.*

Taking Over the World[1]

February 16th

Today, I put my hand into the air
To say, "Yes! I would like to be the one
Who makes a difference in this whole affair,
And those who do not know me will be stunned."
For though, at times, I'm glad to do the part
That no-one wants to do because I'm able,
When I'm at liberty to show my heart,
I'm apt to bring so much more to the table.
Though there are tasks one cannot do alone,
And teamwork will remain its own reward,
Neglect of self is not to be condoned,
And joy in doing's not to be ignored.
When I don't get my way, I do not bawl;
So is it wrong for me to want it all?

---

1. I was excited to be offered an exciting singing opportunity, but fate intervened shortly after I said yes, and I was unable to do it (see "Situational Irony," February 17th).

Situational Irony

February 17th

I should know better than to stand and say,
"Today, I rule the world once and for all!"
Because the world will smirk and say, "Okay,
But please get off that soapbox, lest you fall.
You don't know famine, hunger, war, or need;
Privation isn't something you've endured;
What makes you feel you're qualified to lead
When to adversity you're not inured?"
So housebound now when minor illness struck[1]
I know it would be churlish to complain.
With nasty flu about, it seems like luck,
To suffer inconvenience, and not pain.
And though the world my ego has deflated,
It kindly gave me means to stay hydrated.

---

1. Alas, gastroenteritis.

50

Mocking Bird[1]

February 18th

A mockingbird is not a nightingale,
Although he also sings his songs by night,
With varied voice the world he will assail,
In hopes a mate may on his branch alight.
His repertoire of stolen melodies
He recapitulates without a blush,
And serenades through darkened hours with ease,
No matter how much one desires hush.
Do lady mockingbirds adore the noise
Of car alarms and mobile telephones?
Or does he hope to chase off other boys,
With ceaseless twitterings within his zone?
Through earplugs all the night I hear him cheep,
One wonders when he finds the time to sleep.

---

1. Inspired by John Keats's "Ode to a Nightingale." Also, a noisy bird on a nearby tree imitating a car alarm while I wrote. Those wondering why Harper Lee needed to tell people that it's a sin to kill a mockingbird clearly haven't had a mockingbird outside the window all night long.

Competition[1]

February 19th

Accomplishment and power are on display
Upon a dazzling international stage,
Where medals hang in glittering array,
And myths are made to last a golden age.
But dreams and dedication aren't the key,
They're just a fraction of what gets you there.
And endless practice is no guarantee—
You must have talent that's beyond compare.
But if your schuss[2] leaves much to be desired,
Perceive the worth in things at which you shine.
Do not discount the skill that is required,
My gift's not yours, your genius isn't mine.
And those with unsung skills do well because
Success is unrelated to applause.

---

1. The XXII Winter Olympic Games in Sochi, Russia.
2. A straight downhill run on skis.

Contrariwise[1]

February 20th

On schadenfreude I'm ambivalent;
It may give glee, but leaves behind no peace.
And while it lets old irritations vent,
It breeds new ones that fester sans release.
So when I see a skilled contestant fail,
I'm torn between a wince of empathy
And rattling off some questionable tale
Exempting him or her from sympathy.
It's flattering to think we can decide
If people are deserving of success;
And easy then, their talents to deride,
But it's contempt that's born of bitterness.
There's balance to be found within the shoes
Of those who win as well as those who lose.

---

1. Inspired by Olympic commentary.

Epithalamium[1]

February 21st

When we were wed, it was a civil do,
With ten, including us and celebrant.
And that simplicity I do not rue,
Except one item after the event.
In ancient times, a nuptial song was sung
Outside the wedding chamber for the pair.
From that and Spenser inspiration sprung,
And ten years on, I'll write my own and share.
Now welcome night, and welcome we sweet sleep;
You shoo the dogs away and warm the sheets
While I kick dirty clothes into a heap,
That my approach with grace might be replete.
Our lips meet in that jasmine-scented night,
We sigh in pleasure, then turn off the light.

1. An epithalamium is a poem for a bride's wedding night in ancient Greece, a tradition that inspired Edmund Spenser's "Epithalamion," an ode written for his bride, Elizabeth Boyle. Plus, hey, I didn't get kicked out of bed for the Valentine's Day sonnet, so I figured romance wasn't a verboten topic.

Endorphins

February 22nd

As hunger makes the most prosaic meal
Seem an exquisite feast, so also does
A satisfying workout[1] make one feel
Significantly more than just a buzz—
The sky seems bluer, sunshine twice as bright,
The traffic and the breeze accompaniment,
Within a soundtrack singing of delight,
Reflecting all-encompassing content.
But when delayed exhaustion settles in,
That golden glow becomes a leaden weight,
Enthusiasm turns into chagrin,
Since urgent plans will simply have to wait.
And though the world's not yours yet,[2] to your sorrow,
Take heart that you can try again tomorrow.

---

1. My weekly dance class was especially satisfying after having had to miss the previous week due to illness.
2. Refers to "Taking Over the World" (February 16th).

Old Songs[1]

February 23rd

To hear a live performance of a song
That you remember from a certain time,
It doesn't matter if it wasn't long
Ago, you yearn for it to be sublime,
To sound exactly as it did the day
You first allowed the music in your soul.
So when the opening chords begin to play,
You fear that it no longer makes you whole,
Because the singer's voice is rough and tired,
His high notes do not soar as they once did,
His touring band's quite recently acquired,
He looks like an adult and not a kid;
Yet he makes miracles beyond your ken;
And makes the old song new for you again.

1. Inspired by a video of a live performance by the band Wilco.

On Average

February 24th

I thank the powers for this middling day,[1]
Which started with anticipated tears
That grew into resolve to always play
With creatures that I hope to have for years— [2]
Which made me impotent to rise and leave
For work, when to my lap Giovanni leapt;
But running for the bus, I couldn't grieve
The presence of the dog for whom I'd wept.
I did the necessary things at work,
And musically, I did just well enough
To mask the studying I might have shirked,
Though it was unequivocally rough.
And though the day left much to be desired
Perhaps tomorrow I will be inspired.

---

1. Reference to the poem "I thank you God for most this..." by e. e. cummings.
2. I try not to think about the fact that dogs' lives are so much shorter than human lives.
I don't always succeed. This sonnet was sadly prescient (see "Mass for the Dead,"
January 24th 2017).

Timing

February 25th

Desire can be an inconvenient thing,
That strikes in unexpected afternoons,
Whose sun and scents remind one of the spring,
That metamorphoses into monsoon—
Periphery consolidates into
A self-perpetuating lustiness
Which manifests in focusing one's view
In ways that manners say should be repressed.
But I have the advantage, so it seems,
Of walking through the world without a sign
Of what is going on within my jeans,
The secret fire whose burn is only mine,[1]
I smolder 'til at liberty for action.
Delay shall serve to heighten satisfaction.

---

1. One of the very few advantages conferred by female anatomy. Although, in retrospect, it sounds a bit like a description of venereal disease.

Left and Right[1]

February 26th

As brains and hands purport to show a split
In dominance, so does one's politics;
In habit we're reluctant to admit
How frequently philosophies are mixed.
Such things as privacy and central power
Depend on who's perceived to be in charge
And cynicism all too often sours
Our views of our opponents small and large.
So when some seek the power to deny
The freedoms they enjoy to everyone,
The light of scrutiny reveals the lie
That unfair access favors everyone.
Through principle discrimination mellows,
Engendering remarkable bedfellows.

---

1. A generally dissatisfied sonnet about politics. I was spending too much time on Facebook.

More, Please[1]

February 27th

To my dismay, it's misting here today;[2]
We really could have used some proper rain.
Instead of play in puddles or in spray,
One must negotiate unsafe terrain.
For when in drought, and it is misting out,
The oil and dirt rise, but don't wash away.
So do not shout, if, when you walk about,
You skid and slide, your limbs in disarray.
Though one may hate mist's properties innate,
The way it thwarts umbrellas on the breeze
Is rather great, though it makes one irate,
And mist up noses makes one prone to sneeze.
O playful mist who descends and ascends,
We hope you bring your bigger droplet friends.[3]

---

1. When this sonnet was written, California was in the clutches of a historic drought.
2. This is one of the few sonnets that features internal rhyme.
3. They did! See "Hey Ho! The Wind and the Rain!" (February 28th).

Hey Ho! The Wind and the Rain![1]

February 28th

How I commend you, beauteous, doughty booties
Whose gusset is so firm about my calf
That I may intersperse my daily duties
With splashing and propensity to laugh.
I brace my bumbershoot against the gust,
And when it changes, I adjust my route,
Unlike the passersby, who are nonplussed
To find their brollies newly inside-out.
Though I delight in being well-attired
To challenge our infrequent rainy days,
The weather finds my clothing uninspired
And disapproves in rather pointed ways.
Of windy jokes I find I am the butt
When howling gales blow my umbrella shut.[2]

---

1. From the famous song in Shakespeare's *Twelfth Night*, act 5, scene 1.
2. It really did. Curse you, cheap plastic umbrella frames!

61

March

On Disappointing Productions[1]

March 1st

A past professor[2] once apostrophized,
"Preserve us from directors with Concepts!"
Until today I never realized
That even when design is quite adept,
It's hollow if the chosen point of view,
Sucks out all joy and spontaneity.
Conflicting humors turn the text into
Perfunctory theatricality.
Though challenging a problem play[3] may be,
The most successful moments will be those
Where characters find their humanity—
Amidst the tells, there must be also shows.
Besides, the play was not a total rout;
It gave me something to complain about.

---

1. The Old Globe's production of William Shakespeare's The Winter's Tale was not to my taste.
2. Professor James Frances Xavier Coakley, rest his brilliant, cynical, gentle soul.
3. Shakespearean scholars adopted the term "problem play" to describe his works that are morally ambiguous and problematic. They aren't strictly defined, but plays often described as such include Troilus and Cressida, All's Well That Ends Well, Measure for Measure, and The Winter's Tale.

64

On The Ring Without Words[1]

March 2nd

To skepticism I must now confess
Of whether Wagner's *Ring*[2] could be well told
By an ensemble that does not possess
One singer. When the prelude to *Rheingold*
Washed over me in its entirety,
I feared that choppiness would soon ensue——
Perhaps by cutting out Rhinemaiden glee,
Or lustful Nibelung's attempt to woo.
Though Erda has no lieder, and the horns
Portrayed Brünnhilde's ride,[3] but not her death,
Maazel removes all music of the Norns,
Yet what remains will take away the breath.
Such epic orchestration makes a mark—
One fourteenth of the *Ring* is still an arc.

---

1. The San Diego Symphony's performance of Lorin Maazel's concert version of Wagner's *Ring Cycle*, "The Ring without Words."
2. Richard Wagner's gorgeous, gargantuan opera cycle, *Der Ring des Nibelungen*, which consists of four enormous operas, *Das Rheingold*, *Die Walküre*, *Siegfried*, and *Gotterdämmerung*.
3. The famous "Ride of the Valkyries," which many know as "Kill the Wabbit" from the Bugs Bunny cartoon *What's Opera, Doc?*

After the Storm[1]

March 3rd

The rising sun strikes curls of bark, now stripped
From trunks, and needles dead have browned the grass.
Indurate buds from tender twigs were ripped
As though new growth was torn apart *en masse*.
The shell-shocked trees list t'ward their fallen boughs,
Their heartwood now exposed to air and sky.
Contorted fences, bent but standing proud,
Continue holding green-clad branches high.
In absence of the wind, I hear the scrape
Of rakes that bring detritus into piles
Which then are tied inside a burlap drape
For transport, and then mulching, in a while.
The mulch will bring new growth and keep roots warm,
At least until the next impressive storm.

---

1. Since flora in southern California is infrequently pounded by rain and wind, it sheds dramatically when powerful storms do arrive.

66

What's in a Name?[1]

March 4th

A name is neither tooth nor claw, they say,
Yet there are certain creatures at the zoo[2]
Who are as fun to see as they're to say,
Like binturongs[3] and crested cockatoos.[4]
The bobolinks and bushtits in the trees,[5]
The kudu and the zebu on the ground[6]
In both are kinkajous and mangabeys,[7]
While wombats dig and klipspringers abound.[8]
Yet I should love okapis for their stripes,
And muntjacs for their fangs and tiny snouts;[9]
The mandrill's war-paint lives up to the hype,
And kookaburra's laughs were not in doubt.[10]
A dickcissel[11] exists for every dove—
A funny name's just one more thing to love.

---

1. From Shakespeare's *Romeo and Juliet,* act 2, scene 2.
2. The world-famous San Diego Zoo, where many (but not all) of these animals live.
3. Binturongs, also known as bearcats, are native to Asia. Their musk smells like buttered popcorn.
4. A crested parrot belonging to the family Cacatuidae, many of whom are popular as pets.
5. Bobolinks are small blackbirds. Bushtits are small passerine birds in the family Aegithalidae.
6. Kudus are African antelope. Zebus are humped cattle from Asia.
7. Kinkajous are small mammals indigenous to Central and South American rainforests. Mangabeys are Old World monkeys.
8. Wombats are Australian marsupials. Klipspringers are small African antelope whose name means "rock jumper" in Afrikaans.
9. Okapis are large African ungulates. Muntjacs are small Asian deer.
10. Mandrills are Old World monkeys with colorful bottoms and faces. Kookaburras are noisy birds native to Oceania.
11. An American seed-eating bird in the family Cardinalidae.

Ten Percent[1]

March 5th

I like it when I see the chance of rain
Is only ten percent, it makes me wonder
Which one of ten of us is preordained
To end up soaked and deafened by the thunder.
I keep a weather eye upon the clouds
To see if any might have me in mind
Enough to seek me out amidst the crowds
And spill abundance on me, as assigned.
Who knows what moves the weather to and fro,
Why nations flood while others suffer drought,
Or why one winter buries all in snow
Except in spots where greening seedlings sprout.
When heaven opens, I throw wide my arms
To welcome fortune's sweet, if fickle charms.

---

1. Divisive percentages, courtesy of the Occupy Wall Street movement, were on my
mind when I envisioned some poor sod getting drenched by a quixotic cloudburst.

The Road Taken[1]

March 6th

I took a shortcut shown me by a friend,
And overshot my destination, though
Instead of turning back toward that end,
I chose the distant path I didn't know.
The gate was locked,[2] but easy to slip through,
The road so steep that small steps were required,
But in the elbow of a bend, the view
Demanded to be entered and admired.
Enchantment in the blue of sea and sky,
Audacious squirrels begging human fare,
While surfers slid down glassy swells whereby
The playful dolphins followed them with flair—
The sun-drenched visions filled me with delight
How lovely when the chosen path is right!

---

1. Refers to Robert Frost's poem, "The Road Not Taken."
2. A gate blocks vehicle traffic from the steep access road to Black's Beach from La Jolla Farms Road, though I have seen crazy people zooming down on skateboards.

A Field Guide to Months

March 7th

The month of March, reputed to arrive
A roaring lion and depart a lamb,
Instead, it was a whale about to dive
That made to crush us like a battering ram.
And then the whale dissolved into a flock
Of black and orange monarch butterflies,
Which then solidified into a hawk,
Whose hunting cry was lost in windy skies.
The transformations last less than a day,
Some guises linger barely for an hour—
One can't but marvel at the grand display
And range of nature's metamorphic power.
To call it a menagerie is fair,
As March is madness,[1] I am splitting hares.[2]

---

1. A pun on March Madness, the post-season tournament for NCAA basketball.
2. A pun on the phrase "mad as a March hare," which refers to wild behavior seen in European hares during breeding season and was famously given form by Lewis Carroll in *Alice's Adventures in Wonderland.*

The Genre Game[1]

March 8th

Once, Farce[2] was playing cards with Tragedy,[3]
And both held hands that each believed would win.
While both observed the needed pageantry,
They both were very anxious to begin.
First, Farce laid down a witty dowager
And three fine fops who sought to win her hand,
But countered Tragedy with late monsieur,
So noble that no other could she stand.
Then Tragedy led with her strongest card:
A monarch killed by grieving friend, distraught.
But Farce foiled with absurdity that jarred:
A dozen ways for killer to be caught.
Farce kept his hand with false identity;
And dying breath gave one to Tragedy.

---

1. Inspired by seeing two very different productions in rapid succession.
2. North Coast Repertory Theatre's production of David Ives's *School for Lies.*
3. San Diego Opera's production of Giuseppe Verdi's *A Masked Ball.*

Springing Forward[1]

March 9th

An hour, when lost, is felt throughout the day,
Most obviously at rise and set of sun,
And throws one's timing into disarray;
That chaos never gets described as fun,
For even when one knows the time will change
And resets all the clocks before retiring,
When one awakes, the light feels new and strange,
As though the old and new time are conspiring.
For time's translucence peaks when one can't trust
Circadian rhythms or technologies
Upon which we rely to readjust;
Stress and exhaustion bring us to our knees.
One still takes, in the best scenario,
Half damage from one's daylight saving throw.[2]

1. The phrase "Spring forward, Fall back" is shorthand for remembering which way to change the clocks at the beginning and end of Daylight Saving Time.
2. A pun based on the role-playing game concept of a "saving throw," which is a roll of the dice that determines whether a player's character takes damage from an attack and how much. If the saving throw is successful, the character takes less damage. Of course, reduced damage is still sometimes enough to kill your character.

In Paradisum[1]

March 10th

I tried to enter paradise[2] today,
But then discovered it was occupied.
I hoped the visitors might move away,
And so I lingered some time to the side.
They gave no sign of leaving, so I strode
Amidst the shrubs, conceding my defeat.
Yet those same birds on me their songs bestowed;
The same sun beamed, the same air smelled as sweet.
And from that place, I watched the passersby
Encounter paradise, then stop and gawk,
Desiring that which paradise denied,
Then bitterly continue on their walk.
Such ostentation, lacking privacy,
Suggests that paradise is not for me.

---

1. Part of the Requiem Mass that prays for the reception of the deceased's soul into heaven.
2. In Alexis Smith's remarkable installation *Snake Path,* a coil of the snake's body creates the border of a small garden, which is meant to represent Eden. Since it's one of the few shaded areas in the vicinity, it's a popular place to eat lunch.

The Grossness-Eaters[1]

March 11th

"Courage!" she said, and pointed with her nose
And tail, with lifted paw, in perfect line,
"I sense there, underneath that bushy rose,
The origin of odors most divine."
Then with her scruffy mate the girl did leap
And bury noses deep within the roots.
They there discovered an abandoned heap,
Which tasted to them like the sweetest fruits.
For why should they perform such puerile tricks
For treats when treasures can be anywhere?
Insatiable, no qualm of conscience pricks,
They forage ardently without a care.
They curl up as triumphant memories teem,
Their sated lips a-quiver as they dream.

---

1. A pun on Alfred, Lord Tennyson's poem "The Lotos-Eaters," which inspired this take on the dogs' under-shrub explorations.

Darling Earbuds[1]

March 12th

I am afloat within a sea of sound;
Distinctive whine of engine and the roar
Of ventilation, and from down the ground
The rumble, rubber tires on asphalt, more
Atop it, stop announcements in a timbre
Specific to the driver, and the voices
Of others as around-between, they clamber——
Cacophony: in it my heart rejoices.
And yet the ears around me have been plugged,
With earbuds bringing content on command,
Ignoring their surroundings, as if drugged,
All focused on the objects in their hands.
I don't resent their chosen isolation,
Their music stultifies imagination.

---

1. Wordplay referring to the ubiquity of earbud earphones on public transportation
and punning on "the darling buds of May" from Shakespeare's "Sonnet XVIII."

Lemon Head[1]

March 13th

I spied a lemon hanging on a tree,
As green as the surrounding leaves and of
A height with forehead, and I laughed to see
The danger of a bonking from above.
And every time I passed the lemon tree
I dodged at the last moment to avert
Collision 'twixt the unripe fruit and me,
With its proximity I liked to flirt.
Until one homeward walk in falling night
While half-formed sonnets danced about my brain,
Distracted by these visions, I walked right
Into the lemon. Was it preordained?
As Newton's apple gave us gravity,
A lemoned Libby produced poetry.

---

1. A brand of lemon-flavored candies.

Under Cover[1]

March 14th

"One shouldn't judge a novel by its cover,"
When said by mom, implies the words inside
Convey far more when they are closely read,
Though there are writers striving to misguide.
If, when you crack the spine, you find within
Dishonest arguments, a lazy mess,
It's not surprising you would feel chagrin
Because you lack the context to assess.
And yet, you know your mother didn't mean
For pithiness to outweigh narrative,
Nor does she wish her daughter to demean
Her own desires for this imperative.
Don't let your needs by others' wants be smothered;
To read is one thing; editing's another.

---

1. This is a slightly grumpy sonnet about the way well-intended wisdom can be unhealthily internalized. It's grumpy because I wasn't able to make my original sonnet idea for Pi Day work, though I did manage to force it into existence when I had an excess of creative energy a month later ("Humble Pi," April 29th).

What I Did on My Summer Vacation[1]

March 15th

It started out as every other break,
A hovercraft sojourn to Timbuktu
Where people find it hard to stay awake
Amidst the singing tumbleweeds and shrews.
But on the way, a tidal wave arose
And washed away the lovely waterfall
In which we always liked to dip our toes
Before we caught the monorail to Gaul.
Bereft, with just the contents of a castle
Sustaining us until the thumbs arrived,
We found the native emus to be facile
As through the air and googleplex they dived.
I had to buy a second pair of pants,
When feral penguins I beheld in France.

---

1. A nonsense sonnet about an imaginary vacation, which was written during a very intense period of rehearsals for Verdi's Requiem with San Diego Opera.

A Bee in One's Sonnet[1]

March 16th

As Strindberg hated Ibsen's plays[2] and strove
To set himself an equal opposite,
And Hellman sued McCarthy[3] as she drove
Herself into the grave over the split,
Such passionate antipathy excites,
As legendary treasure does marauder,
And spurs an artist to undreamed of heights,
As Dostoevsky found Turgenev[4] fodder.
But I can't think of any sonneteers
Whose work makes my blood bubble with disdain.
And if I lack those necessary sneers,
Perhaps I should extol and not complain.
Perhaps my writing may elicit curses,
Inspiring someone else to better verses.

1. Punning on the phrase "a bee in one's bonnet," which refers to having a concern that won't go away.
2. Swedish iconoclast August Strindberg hated Henrik Ibsen's plays.
3. After years of political differences of opinion, playwright Lillian Hellman sued writer Mary McCarthy for saying on a talk show, "Every word she writes is a lie, including 'and' and 'the.'"
4. Novelists Fyodor Dostoevsky and Ivan Turgenev mocked and attacked one another's political ideologies.

It's Not Easy Being Green[1]

March 17th

Instead of all the dubious displays
Of "Irishness" that make St. Pat's a bore
I'd much prefer to celebrate the plays
And other works that hail from Erin's shores.
We shall arise and go to Innisfree,[2]
Then take a wake in Dublin, thoughts awhirl,[3]
Await Gogo and Didi's absentee,[4]
And lose the playboy of the western world.[5]
And at the call of Susan's hunting horn,[6]
Duck slippers hurled by angry protégée,[7]
Consider the nutrition of newborns,[8]
And muffins in an agitated way.[9]
A treasure beyond emeralds and gold
Are stories by an Irish writer told.

---

1. In the United States, St. Patrick's Day is frequently observed by wearing green. The title comes from Joe Raposo's famous song for Kermit the Frog.
2. William Butler Yeats's poem "The Lake Isle of Innisfree."
3. James Joyce's novel *Ulysses*.
4. Samuel Beckett's play *Waiting for Godot*.
5. John Millington Synge's play *The Playboy of the Western World*.
6. C. S. Lewis's fantasy series *The Chronicles of Narnia*.
7. George Bernard Shaw's play *Pygmalion*.
8. Jonathan Swift's satirical essay *A Modest Proposal*.
9. Oscar Wilde's play *The Importance of Being Earnest*.

Requiem for an Empty House[1]

March 18th

An empty theater waiting to be filled,
Three hundred voices waiting for their cue
Inhaling dust of cinder blocks yet thrilled
By fervent hopes of doing something new.
Yet while the marshaled forces may impress
Acoustic problems plague the evening's sound,
Despite the vocal power we possess,
Transcendence never quite gets off the ground.
And yet, such great potential lurks beneath
The needful repetitions and parts skipped.
Experience to all of us bequeathed,
The skill of soon forgetting that we tripped.
The stage may change, performers will endure.
Tomorrow will be better, I am sure.

---

1. Written after a rough first rehearsal with orchestra for San Diego Opera's
production of Giuseppe Verdi's Requiem.

Requiem for an Opera Company[1]

March 19th

The speed of bad news through the music scene
Eclipses the velocity of sound,
So when a closure happens unforeseen,
Surprise and consternation will abound.
One's sorrow at the loss is soon replaced
By disbelief and eagerness to blame
Some entity for our civic disgrace
Or else partake a bitter share of shame.
And yet we may take solace in the way
The opera fulfilled outstanding debts;
It took no loans that it could not repay,
It sold no tickets that it might regret.
A company respected by its peers—
Its *Liebestod*[2] moves devotees to tears.

---

1. On the day of our final dress rehearsal for Verdi's Requiem, San Diego Opera
announced that it would be ceasing operations at the end of the season. The
announcement came as a shock to nearly everybody.
2. German for "love death," it refers to Isolde's aria in Richard Wagner's *Tristan und
Isolde*, in which Tristan and Isolde's love is consummated in death.

Requiem for Ourselves[1]

March 20th

Sans opportunity to try again,
With no collaborations yet to come,
Our first and last joint effort will remain
With us, though loss of dreams has made us numb.
So when the house lights dimmed and quiet fell,
Collectively, we had a choice to make:
To let distraction and self-pity quell
The joy of making art for art's own sake,
Or make this singular experience grand;
An evening to remember and discuss
For though the choice was made and we'll disband,
Tonight, we made it meaningful for us.
The peace that met our ultimate cessation
Was poignant as the subsequent ovation.

---

1. The Los Angeles Times called our performance "A stirring Requiem for San Diego Opera's senseless, premature death."

Unexpected Muse

March 21st

A furry interloper has arrived
And laid beside me as I tried to write.
And when I moved, he looked as though deprived
Of shelter on a cold and windy night.
I let him stay, but soon began to feel
The furnace of his back against my leg,
So down the sheets and comforter I peeled,
Adjusting them so that he mightn't beg.
And as I stroked his silky, sleepy head,
I realized my scruffy little dog
Inspired more by lying on the bed,
Than I had written in this evening's slog.[1]
When weary, and one's goal is in the distance,
It's nice to find the path of least resistance.

---

1. Unsurprisingly, I was in the midst of post-performance crash after an extremely emotional performance of Verdi's Requiem. None of my ideas were working until Giovanni decided he wanted to cuddle.

Disappointed Turtle[1]

March 22nd

I see you by the glass, your jaw gone slack
Surveying my prodigious majesty,
Your taste cannot be faulted, yet you lack
Awareness of your own hypocrisy.
When children press their hands against my tank,
Their fingers flat against the curving glass,
Their wonderment's encompassing and frank,
Their innocence will merit them a pass.
A child's esteem does not rise from my rarity.
Whence comes their food, they do not have a choice.
They are oblivious to the barbarity,
By which the careless nearly drowned my voice.
The choices that you make after you leave
May help to give one like me a reprieve.

---

1. Inspired by Eastern Pacific green sea turtles at the Living Coast Discovery Center
in Chula Vista, CA. I couldn't decide if their expressions were peaceful or judgmental.

Bounce and Wag[1]

March 23rd

While Bounce and Wag may be devoted friends,
Each has some strengths and some deficiencies.
When Wag devours food, Bounce condescends,[2]
In time, that food his hunger may appease.
When playing, Wag will zig and Bounce will zag,
They'll bounce and wag, your greeting to announce.
In general, Bounce bounces and Wag wags,
Except when Bounce may wag and Wag will bounce.
When treats are in the offing, both will wag,
And when we go on walkies, both will bounce.
Though Bounce will often try to lollygag.
Of self-control, Wag hasn't got an ounce.
Their virtues are amusing to extol,
Their vices make my tribute to them whole.

---

1. Giovanni and Hildegard, respectively. It's funny that after dramatic events my focus
tended to be on appreciating everyday experiences.
2. Refers to "A Sonnet by Giovanni, a Dog Who May Be Part Cat" (February 6th).

Straight A's[1]

March 24th

If you think it portends invalidation
Of sonnet form to have no variation
In rhyme, you should prepare for consternation:
I suffer from an "ation" word fixation.
Is rhyming A and B a violation
Of scheme, or is it owed appreciation
As virtuosic rhyming demonstration,
Or as a means to build anticipation?
I have such fun with verbal ostentation,
Which well befits my writing reputation,
And listing words that cause stultification
Will help me shun them in communication.
So please forgive this brief pontification
Against the creep of nominalization.[2]

---

1. Instead of using an ABAB/CDCD... rhyme scheme, this sonnet uses an
AAAA/AAAA... rhyme scheme. Inspired by the "ation" game my friend Erin and I
used to play to entertain ourselves while taping down fencing strips for meets.
2. Nominalization is an awesome linguistic term that exemplifies what it is. To
nominalize is to turn a word that's not a noun into a noun, and "nominalization" is
what you get when you nominalize the verb "nominalize." Many nominalizations end
with "ation" (e.g., celebrate to celebration) and are often found cluttering up
academic writing (e.g., heternormativity, characterization, peripherality,
antidisestablishmentarianism, etc.).

Weeping Willows[1]

March 25th

Within the silence, which descends between
The waves of traffic, comes the quiet patter
Of droplets falling softly from the green
To brown ground, strewn with vegetable matter.
Like one who weeps while in the stylist's chair
To see trimmed tresses curling on the floor,
Do trees mourn when their leaves leave branches bare,
Or do they save their tears for something more?
The bleeding bark is cool beneath my hand,
Its scars are rough against my fingertips,
But feeling them, I start to understand:
It's not from sorrow that the foliage drips.
From high above the rough and rushing sweep,
They find the world so lovely as to weep.

---

1. A fanciful sonnet about willows on a foggy morning. I thought it would be nicer than a sonnet about getting dripped on.

Lost Time[1]

March 26th

When I have had my eye upon a goal
For many months and it's at last achieved,[2]
Where once was structure, there is now a hole,
And for those strictures I perversely grieve.
Instead of finding joy in leisure time
I mourn the comfort of the regimen,
And mundane tasks will hardly seem sublime
When dreams of greatness are within my ken.
So any trifling task's an obstacle
Until a bit of progress has been made,
At which point, doing little feels so dull,
And any fears of failure are allayed.
With every step, the path seems less adverse.
Forgetfulness: my blessing and my curse.

---

1. A reference to the English title of Marcel Proust's *À la recherche du temps perdu.*
2. Continuing recovery from that incredible, exhausting performance of Verdi's
Requiem with San Diego Opera.

Better Red[1]

March 27th

Titian, ginger, russet, carrot-top,
Strawberry, copper, auburn, henna, red;
From dull environments bright colors pop,
Unrivaled hues that ever graced a head.
Beneath those flaming tresses freckles spill
Along the neck and down the shoulders white;
A milky way in negative, I thrill
To kiss each dusky star in that pale night.
But how can tender skin remain so smooth
When dazzling fires do blaze so close at hand?
And though there is no answer, I approve
Of multiple attempts to understand.
And over time I hope that I have earned
The splendid privilege of being burned.

---

1. Punning on the Cold War slogan "Better dead than red" in praise of redheads. Or in this case, a specific redhead who didn't object to the Valentine's Day sonnet or "Epithalamium" (February 21st).

Welcome Back[1]

March 28th

Returning to a story that you've read
Brings with it memories of that first time
When you were captured by the tale, although
You know this reading won't be so sublime.
The end holds no surprise, the characters
Can't fool you with dissembling, novelty
No longer has its glittering allure,
Though now it has familiarity:
And while you may recall romantic scenes
Between a lover and his paramour,
You can't recall what happens in between,
And only reading will unlock that door.
Don't be surprised if visiting transcends
Your goal of spending time with your old friends.

---

1. I have no recollection of what book I was re-reading at this time.

Amazing Grace[1]

March 29th

A pelican who yawns while skimming sea
And crashes when his bill will catch a crest;
A fledgling owlet tumbles from a tree;
An eagle lands, but overshoots its nest;
The imprint of a dove in window dust,
When wounded pride's the only injury;
These graceful creatures clearly can't be fussed,
To find amusement in lost dignity.
For them, such gaffes result in life or death,
But thankfully, not even evolution
Can shield from chaos creatures that draw breath;
Perhaps to laugh is mankind's contribution.
And those who watch the antics of the crows
Know humor's not exclusively bestowed.[2]

---

1. Ironic use of a hymn title to describe less-than-graceful moments.
2. The impetus for this comedy of natural errors was answering a crow who was
cawing at me only to realize that it was actually talking to another bird behind me.
The crow gave me the same dirty look as someone annoyed with you for answering
the question they were asking someone through their wireless headset.

Altitude Adjustment[1]

March 30th

To breakfast at sea level then to sup
Eight thousand feet above where you began
And see a cloudy peak when you look up,
Such boundless beauty fills one with elan.
And yet, each step that moves you up the hill
Convinces you your boots are made of lead.
You persevere, of course, by force of will
Ignoring racing heart and lightened head.
Succumbing to that first fatigue results
In curative, rejuvenating rest.
The next day, you shall wake, arise, exult,
If you are not in cardiac arrest.
So take advantage—go outside and play.
A blizzard may blow in on any day.

---

1. Punning on "attitude adjustment," in honor of changing elevation for a week's vacation.

In Memory of a Lost Glove[1]

March 31st

Ascending into chilly alpine air,
Beneath the ski lift, I could barely see
Through blowing snow, a purple object there:
A glove half-buried underneath a tree.
Its palm was facing upwards, fingers flexed,
As if in search of that unlucky hand
Whose owner was indubitably vexed,
To force bare flesh the winter to withstand.
Until today, I'd thought that one right glove
Would sorrow when it went without its left,
But now I understand the right's true love;
Without each other, each remains bereft—
I think that frigid skier would concede:
If you're a hand, then glove is all you need.[2]

---

1. As one whose hands are usually cold, I felt deep empathy for the glove-less skier.
2. Pun on the Beatles song "All You Need is Love."

April

No Fooling[1]

April 1st

I see no lakes from Lakeview Boulevard.
There is no mill around the Mill Cafe.
I will not fall for any old canard,
Especially on this auspicious day.
I wasn't taken in by George Takei,[2]
Whose SNL gig was, alas, a con,
And I felt wistfulness and some dismay
To know Rosetta Stone won't teach Klingon.[3]
And yet, the April Fools are laughing last,
Like Tumblr top hats as a badge of pride,[4]
Or those who thought pet clothing to lambast
Whose canine fashions will be bona fide.[5]
And though from pranking I myself abstained,[6]
I always love a day that silly reigns.

---

1. April Fool's Day is observed on April 1st and celebrated by playing pranks on one another and spreading hoaxes.
2. Actor, activist, and social media maven George Takei announced that he would be hosting Saturday Night Live, which was an April Fool's Day joke.
3. Another excellent April Fool's Day joke was a fake advertisement starring actor Michael Dorn introducing a Rosetta Stone program for learning the fictional Klingon language.
4. The website Tumblr introduced a fake "Tumblr Pro" upgrade on April Fool's Day, which added a top hat to the avatars of those who signed up for it after watching a buzzword-filled but content-free video on what it was. The Tumblr staff soon joked that anyone's account with a top hat was now marked for deletion. However, the top hat soon lost its scarlet letter status because it looked pretty cool.
5. Clothing store American Eagle introduced American Beagle, a clothing line for dogs, on April Fool's Day. But the idea was so popular that American Eagle debuted a limited-edition dog clothing line to benefit the ASPCA.
6. When I published this sonnet online, the words "I myself abstained" linked to the now-famous video of Rick Astley singing "Never Gonna Give You Up." There may come a day when Rickrolling is no longer funny, but April Fool's Day was not that day.

Backhand Spin[1]

April 2nd

Some compliments are lovely to receive;
Especially when softening critique,
But other times it's silly to believe
That some praise isn't nastiness oblique.
If someone says, "Don't take this the wrong way,"
You can be sure that way is what they meant.
"Not meaning to insult you," won't allay
The rudeness and will foster discontent.
A person who would qualify acclaim
With "for a girl" or fears that you won't serve
A good example, knows they deal in shame;
They fight with slow corrosion of your nerve.
And when those pedants fix you in their sights,
Your best defense is stating the forthright.

---

1. A reference to topspin put on a ping pong or tennis ball on a backhand hit, also puns
on the phrase "backhanded compliment," which describes an insult disguised as a
compliment, like "You're smarter than you look."

Ski Ball[1]

April 3rd

It's said a picture's worth a thousand words,
And yet a thousand pictures can't depict
The smell of pine and flashing blue of birds
Against the snowy trees. Words will restrict
The shushing crunch of skis on perfect snow,
The craggy panorama through crisp air,
To paltry meanings of the words I know;
Illimitable Beauty, that's unfair.
The sunwarm bench that summitward arises
Relaxorating, vistious, wonderjoy—
Unloading, turning, suddenawe surprises
With vastness, whiteness, real McCoy,[2] ahoy!
The brightsky blue will fade as cloudrolls near
As we depart: it's all downhill from here.

---

1. This sonnet was written under the influence of e. e. cummings and at high altitude.
2. Refers to Dave McCoy, founder of the Mammoth Mountain Ski Area in 1942 and for whom the mid-chalet was renamed McCoy Station.

Ow[1]

April 4th

Despite my winces whilst descending stairs
As muscles burn from lactic copiousness
Inspiring numerous creative swears
That moderate discomfort do express,
And both my big toenails have gone the hue
Of Concord grapes: impacted, cracked, and sad,
So walking in a thick, restrictive shoe
Is at the least unpleasant, at most, bad.
And yet, I do defy the aches and pains——
I wouldn't trade a bit of yesterday
For pretty toes and moderate chilblains:
There is no joy in doing things halfway.
My thighs may ache, but they will bear my weight,
And though I went all-out, my calves feel great.

---

1. All good vacations must, alas, come to an end. And aches and pains aside, it was wonderful.

Point of Phew[1]

April 5th

Of my opinions I am somewhat proud,
Especially those I've researched thoroughly,
So when I'm faced with one that's merely loud
I'm tempted to engage in repartee.
And yet, a yelling person[2] doesn't care
What anybody else around him thinks.
As everyone is probably aware,
Opinions are like assholes; some will stink.[3]
But even if inclined to sympathy
For what has made a heckler so aggrieved
I find it hard to muster empathy
When I wish he would shut his mouth and leave.
At least some who agreed with me were warring—
No-one should ever say that opera's boring.

---

1. A pun on "point of view," that implies not all points of view are created equal.
2. San Diego Opera general and artistic director Ian Campbell was booed and heckled on opening night of *Don Quixote*, which was to have been the opera's final production, and then the hecklers were booed and heckled.
3. My mother once told me, "Opinions are like assholes: everybody has one." To this I add, "And lots of them stink."

Undeserving

April 6th

Who doesn't dream of cutting to the chase;
Of getting to the callback sans audition,[1]
Or being the sole runner in a race,
Or acting first, then getting your permission.
Such loveliness as being interviewed
For a position that's already yours,
Is pleasant to enjoy, though it is shrewd
To not take it for granted; ask no more.
The minute that you think that you deserve
Those privileges that result from luck,
The just-world theory posits you won't serve
With kindness one who lacks them, hopeless schmuck.
If you don't presuppose a lavish gift,
When it does not arrive, you won't be miffed.

---

1. I was on vacation during auditions for a play, but the showrunners invited me to callbacks anyway. It wasn't a good fit, but I went in and had fun anyway.

Platinum Lining[1]

April 7th

It's said that silver lines the passing clouds,
But science says this isn't really so—
The water molecules proceed to crowd
Resulting in abundant rain or snow.
And yet the cloud has come to represent
Encompassing depression should one fail
Combined with pride one's ego to torment,
And sometimes feels like being hit by hail.
The metaphor is not so apropos,
Since rain, no matter how destructive, brings
Life-giving water to the world below,
And, melting, turns the winter into spring.
So when you can ignore the sting of shame,
You'll find defeat and triumph are the same.

1.To their credit, the show-runners let me know fairly quickly that I had not been cast in
their musical. Given that I really didn't have enough time to be in the show, relief
quickly superseded my stung pride.

102

A Viola Appreciation Sonnet[1]

April 8th

The violin's vivacious, sweet, and wild.
The cello has a winsome, sexy air.
Viola is the awkward middle child,
Whose prospects sometimes fill us with despair.
Violas are so frequently ignored
Because they rarely play the melody,
Yet they give inner richness to each chord—
A voice of understated dignity.
And when it's featured in a composition,
Viola's melancholy, mellow voice
Is twice as joyful in juxtaposition—
Its alto sweetness makes a poignant choice.
Since Hector,[2] Ralph,[3] and Robert[4] all agree,
What's good for them is good enough for me.

1. In response to a Los Angeles Philharmonic concert that featured the Calder Quartet, whose violist (Jonathan Moerschel) was particularly excellent.
2. Hector Berlioz's second symphony *Harold in Italy* features a viola obbligato.
3. Ralph Vaughan Williams's *Flos Campi* is a suite for viola, chorus, and orchestra.
4. Robert Schumann's *Fairy Tale Pictures* was written for viola and piano.

Apostrophe Yes[1]

April 9th

Rhetorical device par excellence:
How Your direct address fills me with glee!
O Universal Cry when fortune daunts—
You all-important hymn of irony;
Reduced in common usage though You are,
To show possession and elided letters,
We wordsmiths venerate You from afar,
Considering ourselves Your humble debtors.
One cannot elevate soliloquy
So powerfully without Your attributes;
Bring into being precious colloquy
Between You and our innermost disputes.
I hope that You don't find it blasphemy
That I've apostrophized Apostrophe.

---

1. A pun on "apostrophe s" in possessive spelling that also refers to apostrophe as the figure of speech in which a speaker addresses someone or something that isn't able to respond (e.g., God, death, love, the sun, humanity, etc.).

A Vogon[1] Affair

April 10th

My uggerblat delivered me a note
All writ in blagcious pildering, which smelt
Of wholded cradgerous, inciting bloat
Which plorped and made each vuvulation melt.
Inveigling proopish fashigoobs with words
Beslavering my varishing physique,
And offering a plungitude of flurds
If only I'd missuage his bludderleak.
But when I folded up this fabberdink,
I saw it was a form ought-seven-two.
My uggerblat was gullfullish to think
That I would gospingbrap a fardelsmew.
I flurked that cobblequirt where it squilked most.
And that's why I now occupy his post.

---

1. Vogons are an unpleasant race of aliens from Douglas Adams's book *The Hitchhiker's Guide to the Galaxy* that are known for being bad-tempered, bureaucratic, and terrible poets. Vogon poets have given the universe such works as "Ode to a Small Lump of Green Putty I Found in My Armpit One Midsummer Morning" and "My Favourite Bathtime Gurgles." This unromantic nonsense sonnet was inspired by Prostetnic Vogon Jeltz's "Oh freddled gruntbuggly...."

How Tweet[1] It Is

April 11th

The World Beer Cup awards are streaming live,
While *Spring Awakening*[2] has its Tweet night,
And *Don Quixote*[3] spectators contrive
To keep the opera open one more night,[4]
My oldest friend quotes *Mary Poppins* lines,
Another, lyrics from They Might Be Giants,
Such fun when to corporeal confines
Technology delivers blithe defiance.
Yet no-one speaks aloud but to be heard
And conversations, few and far between,
Are meant to be remarked on and observed
And do betray a bright, self-conscious sheen.
It can be an encompassing ambition
To court another person's repetition.

---

1. It was a fun night on Twitter.
2. Cygnet Theatre's excellent production of Duncan Sheik and Steven Sater's musical, *Spring Awakening.*
3. San Diego Opera's production of Jules Massenet's *Don Quichotte.*
4. One of many Save San Diego Opera protests which were, I'm glad to say, successful in saving the opera company.

Satu and Son

April 12th

It's worth it to acquire a yearly pass
For visiting the San Diego Zoo
To press your nose against the pane of glass
That separates orangutans from you.
While those great apes are peaceful, dull they're not,
Their personalities are singular,
And to the young ones certain skills are taught
And in new generations they recur.
For Satu[1] learned his treetop acrobatics
From neighbor siamangs,[2] and Karen[3] taught
Him somersaulting, Clyde[4] made automatic
Belief that under burlap's the best spot.
Now Satu has two offspring[5] of his own——
One wonders what they'll pass on when they're grown.

---

1. The orangutan Satu was born at the zoo on March 25, 1995, and has lived much of his life in a multi-species exhibit with both orangutans and siamangs.
2. Siamangs are arboreal apes from Asia, the largest of the gibbons. They cohabit with orangutans in the wild.
3. Karen was also born at the zoo in 1992 and is an open-heart surgery survivor. She likes somersaulting.
4. Clyde is Satu's father, and fond of hiding under burlap. Clyde moved to Kansas in 2011.
5. Cinta, born on March 5th, 2004, and Aisha, born on October 25th, 2013.

Stages

April 13th

This afternoon, I practiced songs I knew
Enough to sing by rote for the first time,[1]
And then this evening, pieces that were new[2]
I read and sang, ambitious and sublime.
Each stage of learning has its devotees,
The first accessing networks that were formed
In practice, and the second, cortices
Newly connected, leaving one transformed.
Particularly pleasant is the vote
Of confidence from pieces you've prepared.
Sight-reading after singing songs by rote
Makes one far less afraid of having erred.
Delightful challenges in great supply,
Make five hours pass within the blink of eye.

---

1. Earlier that day, I drilled memorization for music I was performing with San Diego Women's Chorus.
2. That evening was my first rehearsal with an exceptional group of musicians who were performing Jason Carl Rosenberg's *L.O.S.T.* and Thomas Tallis's *Lamentations of Jeremiah.*

An Extremely Juvenile Sonnet[1]

April 14th

They say the penis mightier than the sword,
But sometimes writing makes one's conscience prick—
It's hard on one to keep one's own accords,
If one does, celebrate with spotted dick—
For cheap laughs are a tool one should not use,
And if you find that door and turn the knob
The package that you find could well amuse,
It could cock up your image or your job.
If your tumescence threatens to emerge,
Suppress it so it won't come to a head.
A shaft of light will baser urges purge,
As Auden or Longfellow might have said.
As triumph makes joy stick to virtue, thus
Our honest manhood truly flatters us.

---

1. Inspired by an extremely juvenile interpretation of William Shakespeare's Sonnet 128, which is actually an extended harpsichord metaphor. Each line of this sonnet contains a penis joke. The best part was that the first comment I received on it was from my father. It was another penis joke.

109

Blood Moon[1]

April 15th

Full moons are lovely but familiar sights.
They cast their gleaming silver and evade
The sharpened shadows of a ravenous night,
Until encountering Earth's umbral shade;
For when most sleepers to their beds' embrace
Succumb, hushed conversations will emerge
When neighbors find their spouses have misplaced
The telescope that passed their latest purge.
My seat's a folded blanket on wet grass,
Our sprinkler-dampened dogs upon our laps,
A strong arm 'round my waist will earn a pass
Beneath that sanguine satellite. Elapse
O fiery moon; beneath the wisping cloud
Your fans find solitude within the crowd.

1. A total lunar eclipse is also called a blood moon because of the brownish-red color
the moon turns when it passes through Earth's shadow.

The Manhole

April 16th

A greensward that I walk past every day,
Contained a scaffold saying to take care,
In my distraction not to go astray
And fall into those innards, now laid bare.
To see a space revealed beneath the ground,
Gainsaying the solidity of sod,
Is fascinating, though it can confound
To see that the familiar's just façade.
And peering down, a part of me expects
To see a caucus race[1] or beanstalk rise,[2]
Thus rendering reality convex,
A world beyond the banal it belies.
And all who seek it shall be crowned the queen
Who rules the rules inside of the unseen.

---

1. In Lewis Carroll's *Alice's Adventures in Wonderland,* Alice falls into a strange land through a rabbit hole. Shortly thereafter, the Dodo recommends a caucus race, in which everybody runs around in no particular direction, in order to dry off after being drenched by Alice's tears.
2. In Activision's 1989 adventure game *The Manhole,* the player encounters a giant beanstalk rising out of the titular manhole, through which one may climb down or up.

One Hundred Seconds of Solitude[1]

April 17th

How fortunate are we to live in times
When libraries exist most everywhere,
Which burst with novels, research, art, and rhymes,
And we can call upon them through the air.
And still, the tactile pleasures of a book
Remain when from a screen your eyeballs sting
And you desire a solitary nook
In which to focus on a single thing.
For when absorbed in reading, one arrives
At space the writer once willed into being,
So even when he dies, a part survives—
An immortality thus guaranteeing.
So seize that part and read it when you may——
Not even death can seal that entryway.

---

1. *In memoriam* Gabriel Garcia Marquez. Title inspired by his book *One Hundred Years of Solitude.*

Self-Compassion

April 18th

On days when tiredness stymies memory,
I do not tax my brain—it is unwise.
I focus on the rudimentary,
The fundamental on which work relies.
And when my voice is tired, I must respect
Its limitations, even though I chafe
To sing full-voiced, I know that to protect
The instrument means shunning the unsafe.
But when I'm hoarse and tired, those double wrongs
Combine to make an exponential right,
Because I know a lot of three-chord songs
Whose range is such that I don't have to fight.
I find it fun to have a brief affair
With singing when I sound a bit like Cher.[1]

---

1. Guitar noodling often results from being tired, as one might be after staying up late to watch a lunar eclipse, for example. I do something similar when I have a cold, which allows me to do a pretty decent Stevie Nicks impression.

Ass Transit[1]

April 19th

I caught a ride downtown with friends, which meant
I made my big appointment in good time.
But when I left part way through the event,
I found my transit options were subprime.
The nearby bus signs showed a transfer point
With my connection just a mile away.
When I arrived, my nose got out of joint
To find it didn't run on Saturday.
Another half-mile to the trolley line,
To ride to yet another transport center
Of which some riders frequently opine
That one who works no weekends was inventor.
For me, it was annoyance, nothing more——
I feel for those for whom it's frequent chore.

---

1. After singing the national anthem for a San Diego Padre's game with San Diego
Women's Chorus, I discovered that the bus I needed to get home didn't run on
weekends. Oops.

Come and Go[1]

April 20th

Abundant and unstructured time's a prize
That slips away from every firm embrace.
One really shouldn't find it a surprise
When tasks appear to fill an empty space.
When needed sleep must cease when it's your turn
To tend to someone else's urgent need,
And food's delayed since you unwisely spurned
Your pantry check and recipe to read,
It all adds up to one exhausting day
In which your modest plans will end up scuttled.
Your inner critic will have much to say
About your planning skills, none of it subtle.
Recriminations, flee this weary head
So it might be productive prior to bed.

---

1. Title stolen from a short play by Samuel Beckett that manages to be hilarious, timeless, and graceful all at once. Personal goal, that.

True Story[1]

April 21st

While wandering today, I chanced on Peace,
Though I did not perceive that it was he
Because he walked with Love, who never ceased
To look beyond his quiet company.
I greeted Love, who knew that I was one
Who knew her kindness well, and so I bent
Receiving ardent kisses in return,
All but ignoring Peace, who seemed content—
But when I rose, Peace held aloft his arm
And folded me into a warm embrace,
While unexpected, I could see no harm
In letting Peace suffuse my private space.
His strength was awesome, then I was released.
When you greet Love, then there may follow Peace.

---

1. This is one of those encounters I couldn't make up. A gentleman I encountered on campus introduced himself to me as Peace. I petted his dog, whose name was Love, and he gave me a hug because he was one of those gregarious people who do that.

Perversity[1]

April 22nd

A lone eccentric caught my eye today
And asked about a poster on the wall.
Demurring, I had hoped to sneak away,
But I had missed the moment to forestall.
He claimed that evolution was corrupted,
How scarcity would lead to civil war,
And scientists whose talks he interrupted
To point this out would then show him the door.
I knew that what he wanted was for me
To praise his intellect and perspicacity.
Though for his troubles I had sympathy,
My pride kept me from speaking that mendacity.
I said that fiction shares his grave objections;
It seemed to me a natural selection.[2]

---

1. An example of my desire to be contrary in the face of presumption.
2. Punning on a key mechanism of evolution.

At Will[1]

April 23rd

Today, I took a dear friend[2] out to eat
To celebrate his birthday, and we drank
To health and love and spouses. Thus replete
With good opinions, in our chairs we sank,
Each falling into quiet contemplation.
I marveled how four hundred fifty years
Had compounded his worldwide reputation,
Yet here we were, enjoying quips and beers.
I wished I could articulate a fraction
Of how his words drew me from solitude,
Soliloquies of limitless attraction,
And verses that my writer's soul renewed.
I thanked him; he accepted thanks with levity.
His wit is frequently the soul of brevity.[3]

---

1. A pun on the name of William Shakespeare, who was baptized on April 26th 1564 (his exact date of birth is unknown) and died on April 23rd 1616.
2. In my imagination, Shakespeare and I are good friends and trade awful puns.
3. Plays on Polonius's famous line from *Hamlet* that "brevity is the soul of wit."

Good Decisions

April 24th

Bleary and sore, I haul myself from bed,[1]
My body moving automatically
Receiving little guidance from my head,
Ablutions thus performed erratically—
My contact lenses weary eyes refuse,
So spectacles elucidate the sight
Of undereyes as purple as a bruise;
A confirmation of a restless night.
As wakefulness begins its penetration
Of murky memory, I realize
I cannot muster self-recrimination
For what my growing smugness does imply.
Though thorough sleep my brain has been denied,
The body claims itself most satisfied.

---

1. Plays on William Shakespeare's "Sonnet XXVII" and "Sonnet XXVIII."

Très Bien Ensemble[1]

April 25th

There is a dearth of concert halls whose sound
Is intimate and gives exoneration
For imperfections that are always found
In live performance; blend or intonation.
So when a first rehearsal brings a smile
To both composer's and conductor's faces,[2]
Not only is the exercise worthwhile,
You have been dealt a hand with all four aces.
And yet, with any group, we're all aware
That anyone could be the weakest link.
And so each person takes the greatest care
To count so that we all might move in synch.
Musicians work quite hard to coalesce
So our performance might sound effortless.

1. Pun about ensemble singing inspired by the Beatles song "Michelle."
2. Response to a remarkable rehearsal of Jason Carl Rosenberg's *L.O.S.T.* and Thomas
Tallis's *Lamentations of Jeremiah* in the recital hall of Conrad Prebys Music Center at
UC San Diego, conducted by Stephen Sturk.

Knowing[1]

April 26th

When we sing chorally, it is a gift,
To all the world, but also you and me,
That's all but guaranteed to give a lift
In spirit to those joined in harmony.
While music to musician will adhere
Inseparable as milk and flour in batter,
Between musicians, there can grow the fear
Of being judged for things which hardly matter.
But when with kindness and profound respect
For differences and similarities
We share a sacred space, we can connect
With gleeful and profound camaraderie.
Dismantling our distrust brings understanding,
Vicissitudes of ego notwithstanding.

---

1. In response to an overnight choral retreat.

Invincibility

April 27th

Mae West quipped, "Too much of a good thing can
Be wonderful," and I affirm tonight
Diverged significantly from my plan,
But nonetheless would seem to prove her right.
The many hours I've drilled each vocal score,
My eyes on the conductor's steady beat,
Might once have made my tender larynx sore,
But no, this night with triumph I'm replete.
Not only did I satisfy each goal
To which, impetuously, I did commit,
I thrived, encouraged, buoyed, and consoled,
And did it all despite sleep deficit!
When my Athenian fire dies down to ember,
That virtue moderation I'll remember.[1]

---

1. I don't even have to look at the next sonnet to know it's going to be about being exhausted.

122

Yay[1]

April 28th

Fatigue makes obvious the energy
Expended in each step of every task,
So even small achievements can bring glee—
In trivial accomplishment I bask:
I won the Prize for Getting Out of Bed
When Dogs Insisted on a Morning Walk,
A Badge of Merit for a Note Misread,
Whose Meaning Was Deduced with Little Talk,
A Grant for Using Sick Days Sans Ado,
A Nomination to Nappers of Note,
Promotion to the Fatuous Sonnet Crew,
And Recognition for Exhausted Throat.
Past heights of my frivolity I've bested—
Imagine what I'll do when I'm well-rested!

---

1. Of my many sonnets about being exhausted, this may be my favorite, if not just for inventing the society Nappers of Note.

Humble Pi[1]

April 29th

Three point one four five nine two six five three…
Point blank for many culinary puns,
Won great attention in antiquity
For making great domes able to be done.
One finds the number inescapable.
Fie on those philistines who dare to utter
"Nein!" in the face of the inevitable,
To overlook the gold that's in the gutter.
Sic erat scriptum,[2] transcendental number,
Fife and drum presage your infinite march——
Thee and I, nonrepeating, will soon slumber
Five fathom full,[3] beneath the heavens' arch.
Ate we the sweet fruits of the ancient world,
Nigh 3-14-15[4] draws; joy unfurled!

---

1. I had the idea to write a sonnet about pi with a digit of pi (or homophone thereof) starting each line on March 14th (Pi Day), but didn't have the time to execute it. I tried to pull off the high concept here, to limited success. Iambs are evil.
2. Latin phrase, usually shortened to *sic*, which means, "Thus it was written."
3. A play on a line from Ariel's song from Shakespeare's *The Tempest.*
4. 2015 was a special Pi Day, since 3-14-15 at 9:26 am embodied as many digits of pi as is possible for a date/time. This won't occur again until 2115.

Daily Farewell[1]

April 30th

O giant dachshund, white blaze on your chest,
Surveying my departure through the glass
Grown hazy from the many times you've pressed
Your nose against that permanent impasse,
Why does my leaving stir such staunch devotion?
Did loyalty and love together spark
Protectiveness? Or did a sudden motion
Betray a cat or bird at which to bark?
Yet in her windowed balcony she sits
Accepting my farewells with stoic mien
Above the door that later will admit
Me to her joyful leap and kiss routine.
For love of sweet exceeding quantity,
Do I respect your varied dignity.

---

1. A sonnet in appreciation of the ever-vigilant Hildegard, who watches from the upstairs window as I leave for work in the morning.

May

Santa Anas[1]

May 1st

O blow, you desiccating desert wind![2]
Wrench limb from trunk and dash it to the ground!
Snap saplings! Sandblast eyes! Crack tender skin!
With writhing branches doors and windows pound!
Your cruelty is indiscriminate,
No ocean breeze can cool your righteous ire
No more than night can force you to abate
Or mercy stay your gusts when you near fire.
Devourer of impenetrable cloud,
You mock the myriad who dare complain
When fog descends to tenderly enshroud
A population that's forgotten rain.[3]
A dream of verdant meadows in a drought
Makes it more difficult to go without.

---

1. Hot, strong, dry winds that blow from inland areas and affect coastal Southern California.
2. Plays on the song "Blow, blow, thou winter wind" from Shakespeare's As You Like It, act 2, scene 7.
3. A slight exaggeration—even residents of drought-stricken California know what rain is. We just don't know how to drive in it.

On Singing a New Composition[1]

May 2nd

As one who meditates must clear her mind
Of vagrant thoughts, so must musicians, too,
Because to notice all we are designed,
And our experiences we accrue.
But like a person climbing up the stairs
Who pauses to admire his innate grace,
Distractions all too easily ensnare,
And one distracted ends up on his face.
So when an hour passes in a haze
Of avid focus and communal bliss,
United in the harmony and phrase,
It's too miraculous to be dismissed.
May none of us forget just how profound
It is to be together lost[2] in sound.

---

1. Our performance of Jason Carl Rosenberg's L.O.S.T. went remarkably well.
2. A pun on the title of the piece, which was a response to Thomas Tallis's Lamentations of Jeremiah. And might also refer to getting lost in the score, but I'd never admit to that.

Pulse for Pulse, Breath for Breath[1]

May 3rd

Rehearsal started punctually at nine—
The sanctuary filled with morning light,
And with the sunbeams voices did entwine
In synergistic, transcendental rite.
And then, my shining raiment did I don
To trip the light fantastic with my troupe,[2]
And after that, I followed a baton
Concurrent with that large and glorious group.[3]
By day surrounded by my loving friends
In kinesthetic joy and aural bliss,
This gentle night, alone, I apprehend
That my mouth's missing one specific kiss.
Artistically fulfilled though I may be,
I long for lover to return to me.[4]

---

1. A line from Christina Rossetti's poem "Echo."
2. My dance troupe performed at a fund-raising event.
3. San Diego Master Chorale's concert entitled *To Music*.
4. Some days, you just want someone to share all the awesomeness with.

Apogee

May 4th

When reading fiction, climaxes are clear—
That moment you've been craving since the hook,
When structure and emotion will cohere,
And justify three-quarters of the book.
So when in life one finishes a task,
The ultimate of any frenzied week,
The structurally aware cannot but ask
If denouement is coming, may I peek?
What sweet reward for toil may I expect?
What kicker may yet zing me in the end?
To what deeds would a bibliophile object?
And may a final judgment yet descend?
Hurrah! My schedule shows doom won't impend
At least until my last gig at May's end.[1]

---

1. Famous last words, especially considering that the following day I decided to sign up
for another audition.

Insubstantial Pageant[1]

May 5th

Imagination: blessing and a curse—
For though it means that you are never bored,
It means your productivity gets worse
If work's less interesting than thoughts explored.
To sink within the boundaries of dream
When seemingly alert and wide awake,
Can make your breathing quicken, eyes agleam,
And feign attention, when you truly ache
For something far beyond the everyday,
Past rote discourse, and bland respectability;
But since the glorious stars in orbit stay,
One might consider dreaming sad futility.
Accelerated pulse may preordain
A change in mastership of your domain.[2]

---

1. From Prospero's speech in act 4, scene 1 of Shakespeare's *The Tempest*.
2. A reference to the *Seinfeld* episode "The Contest," in which four characters compete
to see who can go the longest without masturbating. The euphemism "master of my
domain" was used by the competitors to say that they had successfully refrained from
self-pleasure.

No Rest

May 6th

The Beltane fires have burned, the veil has thinned—
Unconsciously we sense the other side,
And vernal frenzy throws good sense to wind,
As if by work, mortality's denied.
Inspired by nature's blossoming display,
We start ambitious habits once again
And set ourselves new goals, as if to say,
"I should do this, and if not now, then when?"
Alas, I have been caught in Springtime's snare;[1]
It seems that fate and season have contrived
To energize me with delicious air,
Then leave me weary, hot, and sleep-deprived.
There's no rest for the wicked, so they say—
We wouldn't have it any other way.

---

1. I was given an audition slot in less than a week's time and was asked to prepare
challenging excerpts, and it was crunch time at my day job. I replied, "BRING IT!" in
sonnet form.

Woodshedding[1]

May 7th

When I first heard the phrase "to woodshed," in
The context of rehearsal, I inferred
That it meant chipping at a score, therein
Discovering the sounds that should be heard,
Such as an ancient master might have done
To find the form inside a marble block,
And though painstaking work is rarely fun,
To get it right's a satisfying shock.
But no, the phrase supposedly derives
From banishing musicians to the shed
Where of amenities they are deprived,
But they may practice, uninhibited.
Regardless of whose definition's right,
Woodshedding is what was required tonight.[2]

---

1. I learned this very useful expression from Dr. Gary McKercher, then conductor of
San Diego Master Chorale.
2. This was the night I discovered that music I needed to learn quickly was rhythmically
challenging, blisteringly fast, and in a language in which I rarely sing.

Fishing

May 8th

Franz Schubert wrote a lovely little *Lied*[1]
About a fish who frolicked, scales agleam
Until an angler's gimmick did succeed,
In hooking it by muddying the stream.
Sometimes, I'm like that playful little fish
Anticipating anglers' every whim,
But other times, perspective's what I wish,
To keep the world from seeming quite so grim.
So I enjoy my bright, clean tank by day
And venture into riverbeds at night.
Though I've not tired of living thus halfway,
I know, deep in my heart, that I just might.[2]
It's sad to think the prospect of the hook
Prevents so many from exploring brooks.

---

1. Franz Schubert wrote the charming song "Die Forelle" for piano and voice using as text Christian Friedrich Daniel Schubert's poem about a trout being caught by a fisherman. It was so popular that Schubert was commissioned to write a piece of chamber music based on it, which resulted in his famous *Trout* Quintet.
2. Dreams of being able to support myself with creative work.

Sea Shark Major[1]

May 9th

Though you might think that many rows of teeth
And lack of fingers might prevent a shark
From being musical, go underneath
The water and you'll find you're off the mark.
For chondrichthyans[2] know just how to swing,
And all the ectothermic[3] dig cool jazz;
While megamouths'[4] ambition is to sing,
The swell shark's[5] bongos add assured pizzazz.
But if a shark shows up to play your gig
Be sure to give respect as it is due
Remember that great whites are not just big,
They take artistic pride in what they do.
And if you place some value in your life,
Avoid requesting tunes like "Mack the Knife."[6]

---

1. A pun on the key of C-sharp Major. This was inspired by listening to jazz whilst sitting underneath the great white shark that hangs from the ceiling of the Birch Aquarium lobby.
2. Class Chondrichthyes contains cartilaginous fishes, including sharks, rays, and skates. Thank you, Mr. Saler.
3. Animals whose body temperature depends on external sources, like fish and reptiles.
4. A large, filter-feeding deep-water shark.
5. A catshark found in the eastern Pacific. Also a pun on beatnik slang.
6. I imagine asking a shark musician to sing that *Threepenny Opera* song, which begins, "Oh the shark has/pretty teeth dear/and he shows them/pearly white," is as annoying to the shark as it is to be asked to play "Free Bird" when you are not Lynyrd Skynyrd. See "Wassail" (December 19th).

For CAH[1]

May 10th

For years we two have traded birthday verse
Since rhyme and scansion are two skills we share,
And while our challenges may seem perverse,
I like to think we pull them off with flair.
In Limerick, haiku, and even sonnet,
Such subjects as this swiftly passing time
Will be thrown down, we each will muse upon it,
And offer up a piece in tortured rhyme.
Of course, each work is rife with references
To college days and mischief that we made,
How stacks of magazines edge out sax cases
(A quandary that Jeff and I just weighed).[2]
So semiannually my mind descends,
For which I'll always love you, cherished friend.

---

1. A sonnet in honor of a dear friend, with whom I am in the habit of exchanging birthday rhymes.
2. A reference to logistical challenges inherent to expressing mutual affection when there is a significant height differential.

Mum's the Word[1]

May 11th

Despite the fact that first she had my brother,
First born, first son, and something of a test,
She then decided to create another,
And for this bravery she was twice blessed—
First with a blonde-haired infant who appeared
Angelic, but to mischief was apprenticed,[2]
And followed by a lass justly revered,
Whose cleverness and talents were portentous.
Three children who now span the country wide[3]
Whose paths are different, yet display the same
Self-confidence that wouldn't be denied,
And wouldn't be dissuaded from its aim.
Though we resisted being understood,
We still retain her higher sense of good.

---

1. Mother's Day may be a manufactured holiday, but it's a nice excuse to write nice things about my awesome mom, who read every single one of these sonnets in rough form.
2. *cough* Who, me?
3. I'm in California, and my siblings live in Illinois and New York.

Buzz Buzz[1]

May 12th

I speak in breathlessness at break-neck speed,
My thoughts rush out with great rapidity.
Exuberant am I, but now exceed
My normal levels to vapidity.
But this great joy and feeling of inclusion
Is rare enough that I elect to relish
The giddiness, and should it prove delusion,
The memory will be one I embellish:
"Did I tell you about the awesome time
That I remained, just chatting for an hour,
After auditioning—it was sublime
And I showed off my vocal superpower!"
And even if they do not let me in,
I won't recall the evening with chagrin.[2]

---

1. From *Hamlet*, act 2, scene 2.
2. I had a lovely conversation with my auditioners and nailed the prepared excerpts.
However, I will never again choose to do a piece with fiendishly difficult
accompaniment (like "Die Forelle") for an audition.

Little Lamb[1]

May 13th

"Of all the dogs," declared our neighbor's son,
While patting my Giovanni's scruffy head,
"Who live near us, Kylie's my number one."
I've not the heart to tell him that she's dead;
How callous metastasis can devour
Those least deserving of that awful plight,
How miserable to watch its awful power
Destroy a creature made of joy and light,
Or how the loss of a beloved pet
Can shatter elders' fragile status quo.
Perhaps it is a blessing to forget
The reasons it is exigent to go.
I told the boy she moved to Michigan.[2]
He then promoted Gio to number one.

---

1. My husband's nickname for Kylie, our neighbor's sweet dog who passed away from cancer at the tender age of four.
2. Kylie and her owner did move to Michigan for her dog's final weeks. I'm glad we got to say goodbye before she went, but this sonnet still makes me cry.

Revised Expectations[1]

May 14th

A woman who is looking to dispense
With part-time jobs in lieu of one that pays
Commensurate with her experience,
Has got an interview in several days.
Her research shows they have contracts galore
Despite the fact the company's quite young;
She's done good work with some of them before—
She hopes to make it past their lowest rung.
The interview goes well, but at the end,
They cannot offer salaried employment—
Instead, they generously condescend
To offer unpaid work for her enjoyment.
An engineer would tell them where to shove it.
So why is it assumed that artists love it?

---

1. A grumpy reaction to being offered a volunteer opportunity when I was hoping to be paid.

For Pop on His Sixty-Ninth Birthday[1]

May 15

The ERHS[2] class of 'sixty-three
Espoused the phrase, "Make it to sixty-nine!"
And while they might have meant it vulgarly,
It also had a meaning less benign.
For some of them went off to fight a war
In which the country had a dubious stake,
To perish on antipodean shores,
For what was a political mistake.
For those who made it through fate's fickle brushes
Need not recall which sixty-nine's the truth,
Within a dripping woodland flush with thrushes,
While laughing at the vagaries of youth.
There are few men as great and silly as
My very own Paterfamilias.

1. My dad tells wonderful stories about his childhood in our hometown. I'm glad to
share one with numerical significance to the celebration.
2. My father and I both attended East Richland High School.

Burning[1]

May 16th

The grass parched by unseasonable heat
Though irrigated regularly, browns.
The howling Santa Ana winds deplete
The soil of moisture, leaving dusty mounds.
The populace sits on a tinderbox,
Collective breaths held for the winds to change
Thus sparing homes in residential blocks
And shifting the evacuation range.
Cooperation's been unprecedented
Between the numerous fire agencies,
And yet the grumbling of the discontented
Betrays the city's overall unease:
If spring brings conflagrations uncontrolled,
What will the subsequent dry season hold?

---

1. A swarm of wildfires broke out in San Diego County, fanned by hot desert winds, drought, and warm weather. The fires burned at least 29,000 acres.

Left-Handed Compliments[1]

May 17th

When Kirill Gerstein stood up, having played
Rachmaninoff's concerto number three,
More virtuosity was then displayed;
His encore for left hand[2] filled me with glee.
And with his right at rest upon his thigh,
His left spun peerless aural fantasies
That seemed impossible, at least well-nigh,
With just five fingers dancing on the keys.
I thought if Felix Blumenfeld could write
What Kirill Gerstein then saw fit to play,
Such strictures creativity ignite,
Inspiring other artists on the way.
And yet, I doubt there will be much demand
For works like this, typed up with the left hand.[3]

---

1. Though synonymous with "backhanded compliment," I'm literally appreciating a
performance of piano music played with only the left hand.
2. Etude for the Left Hand, op. 36 by Felix Blumenfeld, or at least I think that's what it
was. Initially I attributed the piece to Arthur Rubinstein.
3. I really did type this up with only my left hand. Suffice it to say it resulted in a
number of typos that I did not only use my left hand to fix.

Mood Indigo[1]

May 19th

If I achieve some measure of success
And am invited, then, to sing or play,
I hope that graciousness I will possess
Like Emily Saliers and Amy Ray;[2]
That when I've been performing thirty years
May I still be amenable to things
Both new and different with an easy cheer,
And may I still have voice with which to sing,
For songs of struggle present tie to past,
Objections to injustice tie all who
Believe the songs their conflicts will outlast,
Through knowing that the battle isn't new.
That songs of peace live on is bittersweet—
They never will be rendered obsolete.

---

1. Title of a jazz standard by Duke Ellington, Barney Bigard, and Irving Mills. Also a pun on the rock duo the Indigo Girls, with whom San Diego Women's Chorus performed a benefit concert for the Human Dignity Fund entitled *Songs of Protest, Songs of Peace*. I sang, my husband played. It was pretty awesome.
2. The amazing singer-songwriters who comprise the Indigo Girls.

Gentle Reminders

May 19th

A day that follows monumental highs[1]
That's split between joy and unpleasantness[2]
Reminds one that it's possible to rise
If to the universe you acquiesce.
That stroke of luck that shows you what you need
Before you know that it is paramount;
Awareness of the planting of that seed
Can help you your inertia to surmount.
That vision that allows you to discern
The path between your present and your goal[3]
Forestalls the nagging question if you've earned
The right to drive before you pay a toll.
Farewell, paralysis! Aplomb, hello!
The worst that they could say is simply "no."[4]

---

1. The concert with the Indigo Girls was remarkable. My husband and I kept looking at one another afterward and asking, "Did we just do that?"
2. Refers to a not-wholly-unjustified verbal reprimand at work.
3. Aforementioned reprimand led to a defiant job search.
4. I applied for a job that evening. I didn't get it, but it felt nice to apply.

More Life Lessons[1]

May 20th

If walking shoes don't make your feet feel whole,
For heaven's sake, don't buy them! Don't get pissed
And try to shame a shameless Twitter troll,[2]
Especially if she's a journalist.
When changing purses, don't forget your wallet,
And always keep to-do lists close at hand.
A plug-in dies? Have IT re-install it—
The next time that it's needed won't be planned.
And should an urgent matter slip your mind,
While waiting on another, what you do
When you remember: call her, but be kind—
It's probable that she forgot it, too.
Some days, you reach the point at which you've had it—
You might as well note lessons while you're at it.

---

1. A continuation of "Life Lessons 3,284,925 to 3,284,934" (January 19th). So I guess
it's life lessons 3,284,935 to 3,284,940? Or, you know, just six of an innumerable
number of things that I tell myself to remember but too often forget.
2. Someone who deliberately says divisive and/or insulting things in an attempt to get a
rise out of others who are participating earnestly in a conversation. See "Trollolol"
(August 17th).

I Envy You, Getting to Watch the Show[1]

May 21st

Forgive me, Interwebz, for I have sinned:
I fear that humblebrag[2] I have committed.
Before my Facebook access you rescind,
Extenuating factors I've submitted:
Exhibit A: the brag was full of joy
In shared accomplishment; Exhibit B:
I have invited others to enjoy—
It's all for a good cause (Exhibit C).
Yet, Lordy Lou! I cannot help but grin
At having shared the stage with two rock stars[3]—
The videos and pictures filled with win,
The victory's not only mine, but ours.
Such rapture may be just beyond my ken...
Oh, crap. I think I'm doing it again.

---

1. One of my favorite humblebrags, which operates on the assumption that the person uttering it is IN the aforementioned show and is pretending to be envious of those who are merely watching.
2. A statement intended to disguise pride as modesty or self-deprecation, such as "I hate my Ferrari because the cops always pull me over when I drive it!"
3. Yep, still buzzing from the Indigo Girls concert. Did I mention that they held the door from backstage open for all of the chorus members and wished us well? They're both nice AND awesome!

At the Close[1]

May 22nd

This is a moving-boxes time of year,
When piles of paper stacked precipitously
On horizontal surfaces appear
To cast their leaves away capriciously.
And as shed sheets infect desk after desk,
They settle on the work that's been assigned
And keep appearing, paperwork burlesque,
Resulting in paralysis of mind.
While teachers yearn for summer to arrive
Administrators brace for fiscal close.
What quarters system sadist did contrive
For both to be coevally imposed?[2]
For one tends to succumb to greater tension
When one cannot be granted an extension.

---

1. Refers doubly to fiscal close, the impending end of the fiscal year, and "I open at the close," a riddle from J.K. Rowling's *Harry Potter and the Deathly Hallows.*
2. At my employer, the end of the fiscal year is close to the end of the academic year.

Open Up

May 23rd

When work's intense and sleep's in deficit
A change in schedule can be bothersome;
Annoyance, which resolves into a snit,
Does not those welcome differences become.[1]
For when work's done and sleep is immanent
And music dances lightly on the breeze
One can't maintain a state of discontent,
When sun and joy conspire to bring one ease.
When such gifts come, hold fast to gratitude[2]
For when things will inevitably change;
And with that patient mental latitude,
Experientially expand your range.
And if impatience starts to interfere,
Sit down and order it another beer.

---

1. When I can be bothered to act like an adult when schedules change, I often reap
wonderful experiences, like getting to see family members who were unexpectedly in
town.
2. Spending time with them was, indeed, a gift.

150

Pamplemousse[1]

May 24th

A grand dame, gems a-glitter at her throat,
Smiled down at my and husband's hands entwined,
Remarking on how obviously we dote
Upon each other. Oh, how she maligned
Those lovers who ignored each other's eyes
To stare at glowing screens throughout the meal,
And after eighty-seven years she prized
A life well spent enjoying what is real.
Her words and fragrance lingered in the air,
Approving warmth and *Eau de Shalimar*,
Which left us flushed with pleasure, yet aware
Of shared perspective, even from afar.
While phones may give directions while we drive,
It's sharing love that makes us feel alive.

---

1. We had a lovely meal at the Pamplemousse Grille in Solana Beach.

Roman à Clef[1]

May 25th

Each couple has two origins: the one
They tell their families and then the version
Their friends retell, not just because it's fun,
But also from their own tales it's diversion.[2]
That pair who met "at work" met in a bar;
In World of Warcraft is "we met online;"
"We're high school sweethearts" means he played guitar;
T'was love at first sight? Both had too much wine.
It's easy to dismiss the shorthand tales—
At worst they're trite; at best they are clichés.
But when we find that similar travails
We've all endured, we may just reappraise.
And in due time, we find that we're connected
By incidents and knowledge unexpected.

---

1. Literally "novel with a key," or a true story told in the guise of fiction. The "key" is knowing the true story.
2. Inspired by our friends' wedding, where we and others discussed the difference between how people actually met versus how they tell their families they met. They're often both true, but discrete versions of the truth.

For T[1]

May 26th

Three years ago, a group of friends amassed
To watch the final Potter[2] film together.
Their silliness felt jarring in contrast
To that fell fate befalling their bellwether.[3]
There's not really a satisfying answer
To why such a vivacious Hufflepuff[4]
Should have to battle terminal brain cancer;
Because, perhaps, she's made of sternest stuff.
For laughing wild amid severest woe[5]
Was what she called on all of us to do,
Inspiring us to rhymes most apropos
And many lusty readings did ensue.[6]
And though I never got the chance to meet her,
I know that cancer never can defeat her.

---

1. *In memoriam* Theresa, a fandom friend who succumbed to cancer on May 26th after years of fighting.
2. *Harry Potter and the Deathly Hallows, Part 2*, which was released on July 15th, 2011.
3. While the friends were gathered, Theresa fell ill, and it was then that the tumor was diagnosed.
4. One of the four houses at Hogwarts, the wizarding school in J. K. Rowling's *Harry Potter* books. Its denizens are characterized as loyal and hardworking.
5. From Thomas Gray's poem "Ode on a Distant Prospect of Eton College". I first encountered it in Christopher Durang's play *Laughing Wild*.
6. The tumor affected Theresa's eyesight, so many friends recorded themselves reading stories aloud so that she could share them.

Storied Past

May 27th

It's been too long since I have written fiction.[1]
Though sonnets with my talent set align,
I can't deny my potent predilection
For telling tales of more than fourteen lines.
And so I wrestled with a piece of writing
That previously had given me some trouble,
Whose characters just wanted to keep fighting,[2]
And so my prior efforts I redoubled.
I let myself explore the foolish fancy
Of giving those first scenes a good rewrite.
Though unfamiliar genres can be chancy,[3]
A part of me just knew that it was right.
The fictional inertia has been routed—
And then I had to write a poem about it.

1. For obvious reasons, I wrote a lot less fiction during the sonnet project than I
normally do. It took me a while to get back into it.
2. It's very difficult to write two people falling in love when their conversations descend
into fisticuffs.
3. I wrote a comic book script, something I'd never done before.

Hail to Purple[1]

May 28th

O tree whose bounteous blossoms glow between
The silvered brightness of a cloudy sky,
The sidewalk gray, and foliage of green;
Your vibrancy cannot but draw the eye
In neon violet marching up the hill
You flank the street in perfect parallel;
Prolific panicles that gently spill
Corollas scalloped in a silent knell.
These brief, abundant weeks will end too soon,
As fallen flowers wither, turning brown.
How foolish to ignore resplendence strewn
About you when you fail to look around.
It's easy to take gorgeousness for granted
Wherever jacarandas[2] have been planted.

---

1. Though here the titular purple refers to flowering trees, the title comes from the last lines of Northwestern University's Alma Mater: "Hail to purple! Hail to white! Hail to thee Northwestern!"
2. Jacarandas are flowering trees with vivid purple blossoms that grow in tropical and subtropical climates.

Roughing Up[1]

May 29th

The final word of my initial draft
Can cut like fiery sword into my brain,
And in my frenzy I shall seize the haft—
For editing I'll need its blade again!
For even as I celebrate the end
Of that most painful process of producing
A fiction's fabric for sharp eyes to rend,
Which into criticisms I'll be loosing.[2]
Such skirmishes do not result in wounds
Excepting those that land upon my pride.
But to my faults I kindly am attuned,
Particularly when my brain is fried.
I'll let my story sing me off to sleep,
Regardless of how much of it I keep.

---

1. In my excitement over finishing the draft of a short story, I set a personal record for writing a sonnet: 17 minutes from concept to completion.
2. Once I'm done editing a rough draft to the point that I'm relatively satisfied with it (or utterly sick of it), I hand it off for comments.

Night Drive to Camarillo[1]

May 30th

This journey I am calling quadrupedal
Since over three days it will have four legs,
This scruffy dog I am renaming Wheedle,
For kisses he delivers while he begs.
That dachshund[2] is a desk upon whose back
A halting sonnet I seek to contrive.
The Goodyear grounded under skies of black:
A Giant tethered by the 405.[3]
Of course, sometimes a pithy name reflects
The times that truth became cerebral swirls,
So when I saw planes land at LAX,
My brain supplied the phrase "a string of pearls."[4]
And on such nights I might say poetry
Is saying what the altered mind can see.

---

1. A reference to Harper's "Night flight to San Francisco" speech near the end of Tony Kushner's *Angels in America,* as well as describing the first leg of our drive to Paso Robles.
2. By the time I realized that I ought to be working on the day's sonnet, Hildegard had laid claim to my lap and was reluctant to let it go.
3. Certain freeways in California have such ubiquity and personality that they are given the definite article. The 5 freeway and the 405 freeway are vital north-south corridors for getting through Los Angeles.
4. This memorable description of planes being lined up to land comes from *Pushing Tin* (1999), a film about air traffic controllers.

Phooey[1]

May 31st

One does what one can do, but that is all.
One does attempt to leave none in the lurch.
One aims to issue orders not too tall
So that with failure one need not be smirched.
One tries to take account for human needs.
One tries one's very utmost not to nag.
One to a flagging focus must accede,
For work sometimes resembles lollygag.
And yet, when all consideration fails
To bring about a much-desired result,
One should attempt one's anger to curtail—
Defeat is not considered an insult.
One final drop of patience will I borrow
In hopes that dudgeon dies before tomorrow.

---

1. A grumpy sonnet complaining about a miscommunication that led to me unnecessarily staying up late in order to submit a story by deadline.

June

Unmitigated Gull[1]

June 1st

A solitary gull ignores the water
In hopes that tasty tidbits come his way
From those who crowd the rocks to spot an otter
Along the kelp-choked edges of the bay.
Disdainfully regarding every squirrel
Whose antic japes delight the human flocks,
He claps his wings, demanding their deferral,
And sends them scurrying among the rocks.
And while the opportunists fight for scraps—
Successful scavengers secure survival—
A mother otter croons while wavelets lap
To soothe her fussy, squalling new arrival.
How easily the common coexist
With those on the endangered species list.

---

1. Wildlife-watching at Morro Bay, California. Especially the sea otters.

Positive Reinforcement

June 2nd

When stopping silly arguments[1] results
In finding unexpected things to read,
And when returning calls like an adult
To lovely meals with dearest friends[2] may lead,
And sharing supper with a transient
Precedes escaping my rehearsal early;
Instead of grousing, currying content
In dogs, who spread their joy amongst the surly.
For magical thoughts[3] make us see rewards
In reinforcing certain social mores
When really, there is nothing but discord;
We relish turning happenstance to stories.
But is it wise to censure as naïve
Those things that are diverting to believe?

---

1. We were both late to work because a fatal accident snarled traffic for an hour and a half.
2. My wonderful friend Anna was in town!
3. Magical thinking occurs when someone attributes an event to a cause due to of belief rather than reason or observation, such as thinking that finding a $20 is the universe rewarding you for remembering someone's birthday.

Sonnet 154[1]

June 3rd

By means of online dictionaries paired
With equal measures of tenacity
And stubbornness, for five months I have bared
My life in sonnets for the world to see.
Though my ambitions sometimes fall quite short
Of what I dearly hope they will become,
Whether by concepts I fail to comport,
Or elements that cannot make a sum,[2]
I take some pride in the accomplishment
Of tying Shakespeare's sonnets, just in number,
Though naturally, I cannot but lament
That by his muses I am not encumbered.
Though Shakespeare is the star to my frail barque,[3]
I'm still on course to intercept Petrarch.[4]

---

1. A sonnet in celebration of having written as many sonnets as William Shakespeare did in his famous cycle.
2. See "Humble Pi" (April 29th).
3. A reference to a line from Shakespeare's "Sonnet CXVI."
4. Petrarch wrote *Il Canzoniere,* a cycle of 366 poems, 317 of which were sonnets, about his love for a woman named Laura.

Setec Astronomy[1]

June 4th

When by the wacky vagaries of fate
You find yourself possessed of evidence
That, generally known, would stir up great
Hilarity and laughter at events—
How difficult it is remaining mum
When you just want to holler from on high,
And bite at probability your thumb,
Thus bidding secrecy a fond goodbye.
Intolerable to have fire within
That must needs suffer from asphyxiation—
To tell is disappointment and chagrin;
Maintaining silence brings no consolation.
Though indiscretions make their cases well,
I hold my tongue, though tales it longs to tell.[2]

---

1. An anagram for "too many secrets," which comes from the 1992 film *Sneakers*.
2. I couldn't share a delightful synchronicity between a story I'd written and a story unfolding in the wider world due to a disparity in publication dates.

Craft[1]

June 5th

It's pleasurable to take a single word
And craft a couplet that conveys a thought
That won't seem obvious or too absurd,
And won't result in language overwrought.
So when a thought's expressed in prosody
That mimics a vernacular expression,
By means of dictional simplicity,
That stylish choice can cloud lines of succession—
For oh, delicious diction of the past,
Thou still unravish'd lexicon of plums,[2]
Your toothsomeness would make a fine repast
If next to you I did not feel so dumb.
Poor fingers that must trudge across the keys,
Have faith you will convey a greater ease.

---

1. Given the number of sonnets I wrote, I'm surprised so few of them are actually about writing sonnets.
2. A reference to John Keats's "Ode on a Grecian Urn."

Grr[1]

June 6th

Through growling grogginess I do perceive
A growing groundswell of determined grit
To grab with gruffness, nevermore to grieve
For time lost as in gridlock gross we sit.
Grandiloquent is our collective grouse,
With gravitas our grievances we air,
We grapple with regret for leaving house,
Exchanging the most gratifying glares.
It's said that misery loves company,
But on gray days, we're all of us annoyed,
Our solitary grumps will trump any
Enjoyment that results from schadenfreud'.
Yet Friday brings a pleasant turnabout
When our sun can be bothered to come out.

---

1. Wordplay on the onomatopoeia derived from a growl, which is also the featured consonant cluster.

The Cliff

June 7th

The first activity in several weeks[1]
That works to stretch the body and the mind
Is sure to put some roses in one's cheeks
And afterward will help one to unwind,
Endorphin clouds in which the body drifts,
The muscles loose, the brain demanding naps,
All make one blissfully oblivious
To imminent and foreordained collapse.
When it arrives, it turns the brain to lead,
Joints crack and new-found aches confirm contusion,
While stiffness spreads through shoulders, neck, and head,
Attempts at cogent thought end in confusion.
Though creativity exhaustion quells,
At least I can expect to sleep quite well.

---

1. Inspired by my first dance class in several weeks, having missed several due to company and travel.

Least of All Possible Evils[1]

June 8th

When deadlines change from three weeks into one
Priorities must then be rearranged:
Allot the maximum that can be done
And hope that no one task will be shortchanged;
For when there are three tasks, and two of them
Involve a partner, you'll be glad you worked
The solo parts: strategically condemn
The group and hope the partner hasn't shirked.
But destiny ignores all strategy,
No matter how meticulously planned
And so whatever outcomes you foresee,
Prepare for their dismissal out of hand.
Through work and luck, at best you may have pieced
A stratagem by which you lose the least.

---

1. A play on Dr. Pangloss's famous credo from Voltaire's *Candide.*

Fifty Meter Freestyle[1]

June 9th

With plays and verses Shakespeare did decree
The iamb[2] as the undisputed king
Of metered feet, disdaining the spondee[3]
And anapests[4] to make his poems sing.
Verses sound unbalanced with a trochee[5]
Swapped for every iamb, feet left over,
And lines that are all spondees must be
Bland stuff that could not urge one's heart to stir.
But of course there are meters more graceful that naturally dance
And the anapest brings us sweet memories, childhood in rhymes,
Dactyls,[6] by contrast, intensities always enhance
Driving inexorably to the ends of the lines.
This raises but one question: ponder on it.
If not comprised of iambs, is it sonnet?

---

1. A pun on the name of a swimming event that humorously exaggerates my attempt to fit as many types of metrical feet into this sonnet as possible.
2. An iamb is a disyllable in which an unstressed syllable is followed by a stressed syllable, as in the word "compare." The first stanza and final couplet are written in iambic pentameter.
3. A spondee is a disyllable with two equally stressed syllables, such as the word "childhood." The last two lines of the second stanza are written in pentameter featuring spondees.
4. An anapest is a trisyllable comprised of two unstressed syllables followed by a stressed syllable, as in "comprehend." The first two lines of the third stanza are written in anapestic pentameter.
5. A trochee is the opposite of an iamb, a disyllable comprised of a stressed syllable followed by an unstressed one, like the word "chosen." These two lines are written in trochaic pentameter.
6. Dactyls are trisyllables of one stressed syllable followed by two unstressed syllables, like the word "merrily." These two lines are written in dactylic pentameter.

Summarize Proust[1]

June 10th

My seatmate said, "That book is pretty big—
What's it about?" I truly wish I knew
How to describe without seeming a prig
Marcel Proust's *À la recherche du temps perdu*.[2]
"The longest, greatest novel ever written?"
"Reflections on names or shifting perceptions
That chronicle the joy of being smitten
By literature and love at its inception?"
"The book my friend and I had planned to read
The summer he abruptly passed away,
Thus kindling in me an impassioned need
To savor every volume past *Swann's Way?*"[3]
For reasons far too numerous to state,
I smiled at him and said, "It's really great!"

---

1. Refers to a *Monty Python's Flying Circus* sketch about an All-England Summarize Proust competition in which the contestants compete to see who can summarize the most of Marcel Proust's novel *À la recherche du temps perdu* in fifteen seconds. The contestants fail to get past the first section of the first book.
2. The novel, which spans seven volumes, is one of the longest in western literature. It's over three thousand pages long and contains over 1.2 million words.
3. My friends Nathan and Christine and I planned to read the work in its entirety together, but Nathan passed away unexpectedly the summer we started Volume 1, *Swann's Way*.

Le Pew[1]

June 11th

When through the open window evening breeze
Delivers a distinctive sort of funk,
I know that for some time I'll take my ease
Surrounded by the stink of *eau de skunk.*
Inhaling that distinctive sulfurous scent,
Reminds me of my childhood when a whiff
Of woodland musk inevitably meant
That with a skunk our dog had had a tiff.
I'm now convinced that each skunk adolescent
Selects my street for his initiation
To cross the lanes when traffic is incessant,
Which all too often leads to ruination.
Their fates were written by the moving finger,[2]
But, thanks to their biology, shall linger.

1. Refers to the Loony Tunes/Warner Bros./Merrie Melodies cartoon character Pepé le
Pew, an amorous skunk with an exaggerated French accent (voiced by Mel Blanc and
Maurice LaMarche) who terrorizes cats that he mistakes for lady skunks.
2. A reference to the *Rubaiyat* of Persian polymath Omar Khayyam. Edward FitzGerald
famously translated Khayyam's quatrain about fate as "The Moving Finger."

Tried Patience, or, Happy Birthday, Mom!

June 12th

O Sainted Ellen of the Grillèd Cheese:[1]
You fed the hungry lunch in bright array,
Our childish apprehensions did you ease,
And with your laughter banished our dismay,
And with a bowl, as first donned by St. Loony
Of Monty Python fame,[2] upon your head
Made golden halos seem supremely puny,
Declaring naughty words could now be said.
Irreverence isn't singular among
Your virtues; kindness, fearless curiosity,
Inspire us to sing what was unsung
And emulate your thoughtful generosity.
I only hope my life will be as filled
With fun at which I hope I'll grow as skilled.

---

1. My mother's nickname among my high school friends for the superb sandwiches she made for us when we came home from school over the lunch hour.
2. A reference to a sketch in *Monty Python's Flying Circus*, Episode 36, featuring St. Loony Up the Cream Bun and Jam.

Purpose Full

June 13th

I have forgotten what it's like to lack
A deadline looming just around the bend.[1]
Accustomed now, I'm quite taken aback
When there's no challenge that I should transcend.
My mind feels stagnant when I do not write,
And sluggish at those times I do not read,
Or work up well-loved poems to recite,
And scores to sing, the old to supersede.
I wonder if my patent inability
To be without new projects is a skill
Or failing—either is a possibility
For work itself is neither good or ill.
As long as my enjoyment outweighs stress
I'm grateful for the freedom to digress.

---

1. I forget this way more frequently than I would care to admit.

The Finch Response[1]

June 14th

Galapagos's tortoises maintain
A fascinating reflex when a bird
Alights upon them, it's as if the brain
Declares all other stimuli deferred—
They haul their massive carapaces high
As short and stump-like legs will them allow,
With necks upraised, all forces to defy,
Still as a figurehead on frigate's prow.
This unresponsive state lets native finches
Pick off the shedding skin and parasites
Upon its most discriminative inches
Sans inadvertent startling into flight.
Yet sleep's descent I cannot yet allow
While wings of inspiration brush my brow.

---

1. Named for the fascinating physiological response that the Galapagos tortoise keepers demonstrated in a special presentation for San Diego Zoo members.

Night Stroll

June 15th

Come walk beneath a thousand blazing suns
Whose distance renders them to sparkling points
And let the moistened grasses when we run
With fallen dew my sandaled feet anoint.
Let constellations witness our escape
From suffocating confines of the home,
The lucent firmament will make us gape,
Its shifting beauty guides us as we roam.
You comprehend the reason for our tryst
Amidst the starlit, jasmine-scented night——
The tender skin behind my knee you kissed,
Your eyes sought mine, the stars weren't half as bright.
And then you squatted, I produced a bag,
You led us home, your tail all a-wag.[1]

---

1. I can't really call this an anti-romantic sonnet because nighttime dog walks can be
lovely, despite the walk's *raison d'être*.

174

Surprise[1]

June 16th

I'm glad I cleared my schedule for a day
So when assignments suddenly appeared
They caused me but a moment of dismay
Before I girded loins and volunteered.
Farewell, sweet slack and idleness of mind!
Adieu commuting hours with Marcel Proust!
Here cheer and masochism are combined,
As by adrenaline I am seduced.
But even if I manage to complete
All tasks within the meager time allowed,
Perhaps the victory won't taste as sweet
If of my slapdash efforts I'm not proud.
Perfection may well be the foe of done,
But mediocrity is never fun.

---

1. I call this the Law of Spontaneous Task Generation. Nature abhors a scheduling vacuum, so whenever there appears to be a block of free time, a task will suddenly appear and consume the entirety of the free time.

The Fail Cycle[1]

June 17th

To be aware you've been set up to fail
Does not make failing any easier.
Entreaties may be from beyond the pale,
But asker's confidence it will occur
Infects your brain and makes you wonder why
You hesitated just before agreeing.
Now you've agreed to give the task a try,
Your self-recrimination guaranteeing.
It breaks the heart so nearly to succeed
When in the shared delusion you've invested
Your time and worked until your fingers bleed,
For failure finds your faith in self arrested.
And so the next time chutzpah comes your way
You're likelier to shrug and say okay.

---

1. I was already regretting accepting the assignment a mere two days into the ten I had to complete it. Fortunately, I'd started on it early. The results fit the requirements, which is about the most one can hope for in such circumstances.

Take the Cake[1]

June 18th

O jammed *genoise* whose silken chocolate coat
Breaks crisply and then melts upon the tongue
And radiates its warmth all down the throat,
For decades has your loveliness been sung;
The Jaffa Cake, throughout the world renowned,
Almost fell victim to its own success——
Initially, a tax tribunal found
The cakes were biscuits, but there was redress:
Though they seemed similar when side-by-side
A court deemed cakes distinct from biscuitkind,
And strict criteria were then applied
That future cakes need not be redefined.
But just in case, I now submit my fitness
For future challenges, to be a witness.

---

1. A paean to Jaffa cakes, that delicious delicacy my best friend's English mother was
always sure to have in the house (a fact I appreciated often).

'Tis the Saison[1]

June 19th

Pete Seeger's song says that to every thing
There is a season,[2] so when I do drink
A lovely beer, its praises I will sing
As of its taste and timeliness I think—
For when the sun shines hot, then hops I crave,
As in the winter I love Christmas ale.
For fall, Oktoberfest bier I will save,
And in between, saisons will never fail
To bring delight, yet one cannot but wonder
How spring and autumn beverages unite,
Though one would think they'd steal each other's thunder
Engaged in world's most satisfying fight.
Deliciousness may be the only trait
From which saisons should never deviate.

1.A sonnet about the saison, a fruity, spicy style of farmhouse beer that originated in
French-speaking Belgium. The name is French for "season."
2. Pete Seeger's song "Turn! Turn! Turn! (To Everything There is a Season)," which was
made famous by the Byrds, featured text adapted from the third chapter of Ecclesiastes.

Refilling the Well

June 20th

When asked to write a story in ten days
The only way that I know to succeed
Is stealing bits of time from work and play,
And then converting them to what I need.
But by the time the story is submitted,
The spring of inspiration has run dry;
To prime the pump is merely not permitted,
It's needful to maintain the mind's supply.
And so my eyes devoured each luscious word
That it was in my power to provide,
And yet the brain commands me, undeterred,
To read until it may be satisfied.
I'm grateful to receive a mental boost
Each time I read a paragraph of Proust.[1]

---

1. I was reading Volume 3, *The Guermantes Way*, at the time. See also "Summarize Proust" (June 10th).

Grow Up

June 21st

When children wish that they were fully grown
Adults will scoff and say they should enjoy
The carefree years before they're on their own.
Such sentiments are certain to annoy,
For there's a fundamental misconception
That toys and sweets are what they would possess.
Yet by that age, they're sure to take exception
To inequality without redress.
For what adult has never felt frustration
At being overlooked or even taunted
When seeking dominance and approbation?
Is this a thing to which one should be wonted?
Besides, ice cream for meals brings finite cheer
Since many flavors do not go with beer.[1]

---

1. This is one of the more important lessons of adulthood.

Necessarily So[1]

June 22nd

B minor is the key that Gershwin chose
For his sublime creation "Summertime."[2]
But for a previous singer someone chose
A full C minor chart; hardly a crime.
A half-step up makes little difference
To saxophones in their ideal range,
But for a vocalist, it shows us whence
A lovely piece can end up sounding strange.
And so a song that sits high in the voice
Becomes unsingable when raised a jot
And so we get to make the lousy choice
To sing a seventh down or sing it not.[3]
At least when I arrive at the reprise,
I'm free to sing whatever notes I please.

---

1. Refers to the George Gershwin tune "It Ain't Necessarily So" from *Porgy and Bess.*
2. Clara's famous lullaby from *Porgy and Bess.*
3. It's not fun having to sing in a key that doesn't suit your voice.

Similes Like Metaphors[1]

June 23rd

When someone called me poet, I demurred
And said that what I write is really verse;
When asked the difference, memory deferred
To dictionary, lest I make things worse.
I found that verse has meter, which I knew,
And often features rhymes at ends of lines,
And while a poem has a rhythm, too,
It's figurative language that defines.
So if some standard verse I wish to write,
I'll stick to my familiar metric feet.
But if a poem's in the cards tonight,
There's just one thing it needs to be complete.
To call this verse when it is poetry;
Could that be classified synecdoche?[2]

---

1. Wordplay involving the definition of a simile, a literary comparison that uses "like" or "as," and a metaphor, a literary comparison that does not.
2. A figure of speech in which the whole is represented by a part of that whole, such as referring to a car as "wheels."

Argument Clinic[1]

June 24th

On days when fights are easier to pick
And one must call on friends to whine and vent,
Some time detached from conflict is the trick,
Since fury flooding further strife foments.
So moments spent with meals or taking walks
Could re-align perspective and revive
One's absent humor, though attentive talks
Can keep the heated bickering alive.
But when the mind has truly disengaged,
Then memories the mind may then enthrall—
While there's no room for them when one's enraged,
In peace, the brain finds what the heart recalls.
The anniversary of dear friend's passing[2]
Shall raise recurring ripples everlasting.

---

1. Reference to another *Monty Python's Flying Circus* sketch in which a man walks into an office looking for an argument and proceeds to argue about the quality of the argument he receives.
2. Death anniversaries affect us, whether we're conscious of them or not.

On Othello[1]

June 25th

Though Hamlet's *Mousetrap*[2] shows a regicide
By deadly poison dribbled in the ear,
Far crueler is toxicity implied
By cunning tongue believed to be sincere,[3]
A weapon won't discriminate; a knife
Will slay without regard for class or wealth,
But slander visited upon a wife
Is vile attack by proxy via stealth.
For Shakespeare knew the greatest tragedy
Was hurting those whose standings were precarious
By goading paramours to jealousy;
The innocent destroyed by the nefarious.
Four hundred years ago he understood
That bad thoughts grow more easily than good.

---

1. In response to the Old Globe Theatre's production of Shakespeare's *Othello*.
2. The play-within-a-play that Hamlet contrives to determine Claudius's culpability for Hamlet's father's death, about which Hamlet famously says, "[T]he play's the thing wherein I'll catch the conscience of a king."
3. Refers to Iago, the villain who takes it upon himself to convince Othello that his faithful wife Desdemona is cuckolding him with one of his officers.

Always Playing

June 26th

Road trip vacations could have been the worst,
But we had Stinky Pinkies[1] and Padiddles[2]
With trucker honks[3] and I Spy[4] interspersed,
And in the desperate times, we played at riddles.
But as we grew, our games also matured
To "In My Pants"[5] and "Who'd You Rather Kiss?"[6]
But from these callow pastimes I was lured
By golden promises of lasting bliss.
For when I first heard Yellow Car[7] described,
In which the yellow cars are pointed out
With non-car targets thoroughly proscribed;
A never-ending, never-winning bout—
As long as people drive, then here we are
Forever always playing Yellow Car.[8]

---

1. A word game in which players take turns inventing clues whose solutions rhyme. For example, "A corpulent feline" would be a fat cat.
2. A car game in which the first person to see another car with one burned-out headlight yells "Padiddle!" Depending on the rules of the car, one may have to hit the ceiling of the car or earn the right to punch a fellow passenger.
3. When car passengers make a chain-pulling gesture at semi-trailer truck drivers s on the road to request that the driver blow his or her air horn.
4. A guessing game in which players take turns saying, "I spy with my little eye something beginning with [the letter that starts the object the player has chosen]." This can be an exceptionally boring game to play in the car.
5. A game in which players read roadside signs aloud and add the words "in my pants" to the end for comic effect.
6. A game in which players take turns asking "Who would you rather kiss?" and offer a choice of two potential kiss-ees. The rules are described more completely in "The Great Game" (July 21st).
7. A game that consists of saying "Yellow car!" when you see a yellow car, as described in the "Ottery St. Mary" episode of John Finnemore's BBC Radio 4 comedy series *Cabin Pressure.*
8. According to the game's inventor, there is no way to win at Yellow Car, but you're always playing.

185

Jump, Dive, and Whale[1]

June 27th

A whaling voyage loomed within the cards,[2]
And having little wealth with which to hire
Harpooners, smiths, or doughty foc's'le tars,
We set to sail, our fortunes to acquire.
But what fair wind 'twas started at our backs
Soon chilled our hot pursuit clear to the bone.
Inadequate our floundering attacks,
Until I faced fell Timor Jack[3] alone.
Such early victories are often Pyrrhic,
But this time, fickle fortune smiled on me,
For once, the chapter Symphony[4] was lyric
Instead of pitiless as shark-filled seas.
The Pequod sank in her pelagic grave,
And I, not Ishmael, was somehow saved.

---

1. A pun on Louie Prima's song "Jump, Jive, an' Wail."
2. This sonnet was inspired by a game of King Post's excellent *Moby Dick, or, The Card Game*, which follows the plot of Herman Melville's famous novel and always begins with the book's opening chapter, "Loomings."
3. A notorious historical whale that Melville mentioned in *Moby Dick* as "scarred like an iceberg" from fighting off numerous attacks by whalers. When he appears in the *Moby Dick* game deck, he usually escapes after killing your boat crew. But if you take him, you receive a bonus for the rest of the game.
4. As you proceed in the card game, different chapters of the book come up and affect the game play. The Symphony is a particularly brutal chapter, because every sailor who falls into the sea during the frequent whale hunts is eaten by sharks instead of returning to the sailor deck, where he can be hired again.

Perfection Protocol

June 28th

Just who can say what makes a splendid day?
Could it be weather, neither gray nor sunny?
Or lovely friends, or impromptu soirées
At which a game predictably turns funny?
Or maybe it's that mix of novelty
And mourning those familiar things now past,
Although some aspects of the memory
Persist, despite unlikeliness to last.[1]
Perhaps these complications and desires,
Thus born of what's expected and believed,
Engender joy that naturally transpires
When perfect parity has been achieved.
The confluence of wistfulness and verity
Are sadly, an inestimable rarity.

---

1. I was definitely reading Proust when I wrote this.

Calibration

June 29th

When asked to do a task that one will fail,
And no-one else could possibly fail less,
To acquiesce and know one won't prevail,
Will always hope of better things depress.[1]
When bearing blows for others is the norm,
Perceived a toll for traveling the road,
Conditioned thus, it seems to be bad form
To point out the disparity in load.
So when new leadership makes a request
On finding to what you're habituated,
That one speak up when one is feeling stressed,
With dreams of normalcy one's inculcated.
Alas, while old assumptions will persist,
The status quo and hope can't coexist.[2]

---

1. I lived every singer's nightmare: having to get up and sing a solo that I didn't know because none of the other singers knew it, there was no vocal score or lead sheet, nobody could tell me what the changes were, and nobody with that information cued me. It wasn't fun, but at least having lived it, it no longer terrifies me as much.
2. I knew I wasn't going to be singing with the band for much longer because rehearsals for *Hunchback of Notre Dame* were starting in August.

Halfway[1]

June 30th

It isn't easy finding time to write
In every day, regardless of demands
Upon your mental bandwidth and despite
Dismissal from those who misunderstand
The freedom that exists in structured tasks,
Such as the ritual of sitting still
And giving yourself latitude to ask,
"If this word doesn't work, then which one will?"
I wouldn't call it discipline—perhaps it
Is something in the satisfaction of
Creating things; Perhaps it's even habit—
But at its root, it's doing what you love.
So in successes, bask in jubilation
And try to overlook sleep deprivation.

---

1. In celebration of making it halfway through the yearly sonnets.

July

Silencing Chihuahuas

July 1st

An influential pedagogue[1] describes
Those voices of self-doubt that plague one's sleep
"Chihuahuas," whose incessant yips and gibes
Convince one that the price of action's steep,
Resulting in paralysis, despair,
Depression, paired with self-effacing fevers.
The only cure of which I am aware:
Replace Chihuahuas with Golden Retrievers.[2]
"You ought to hate yourself, but I love you!"
"You could do better, still, you're my best master!"
"That thing you keep forgetting you should do
You will do. Now please toss my duck toy faster?"
Self-loathing cannot but face a deferral
When it's accompanied by cries of "Squirrel!"[3]

---

1. Members of the Metro Theatre Company in St. Louis, who were instructors at Illinois Summer School for the Arts (integrated arts camp!).
2. This idea came from a conversation with my friend Amelia about how to work through adversity by replacing the critical inner voices with kinder ones.
3. A reference to Dug, an affectionate but easily-distracted golden retriever in the Pixar film *Up.*

A Tale of Honey[1]

July 2nd

A poet sees the flower as a sign
Of transience, and beauty that will fade,
But to a plant, a blossom's fair design
Ensures its pollinators will be stayed.
And pollinators, heedless of the part
They play in reproduction, blindly seek
To take their tithe of sweetness and depart;
No poetry the process would bespeak,
Unless one thinks of honey, and the bees
Who perishable nectar do devour,
And metamorphose it with seeming ease
To that which never spoils[2]—whence came this power
To change mortality to perpetuity?
An evolutionary superfluity?

---

1. A play on the title of the Beatles song "A Taste of Honey."
2. Due to honey's acidity and low water content, which inhibits the growth of bacteria and fungi, honey doesn't go bad. We have edible samples of honey that are over 3,000 years old. Honey does, however, crystallize, but can be reconstituted in warm water.

Putting Words into His Mouth[1]

July 3rd

While Shakespeare wrote innumerable lines
That have forever changed our lexicon,
Too often one mistakenly assigns
A phrase to him that must then be withdrawn.
He did not ask what tangled web we weave
When first we practice to deceive— that's Scott.[2]
No man's an island— this you may believe,
But Donne[3] it is, and Shakespeare it is not.
Poor Congreve,[4] Milton,[5] Marlowe,[6] Franklin,[7] Browning[8]—
Whose pithiness shall ever be dispensed
By generations who insist in crowning
Will Shakespeare King of Wit at their expense.
At least, perhaps he has some competition
From Oscar Wilde[9] in piquant erudition.

---

1. This was inspired by a mistake of attribution I made, which led down a highly entertaining internet rabbit hole.
2. From *Marmion* by Sir Walter Scott.
3. From John Donne's poem called, appropriately enough, "No Man Is An Island."
4. William Congreve's play *The Mourning Bride* is the source of the old chestnut about hell having "fury like a woman scorned," which is often attributed to Shakespeare.
5. "Better to reign in hell, than to serve in heav'n," and many other lovely lines from Milton's *Paradise Lost* have been attributed to Shakespeare.
6. Christopher Marlowe's poem "The Passionate Shepherd to his Love" is full of language that Shakespeare might have written but didn't, particularly the refrain "Come live with me and be my love."
7. Though "Time is money" sounds like it could have come from Polonius, the aphorism came from Benjamin Franklin.
8. Elizabeth Barret Browning's *Sonnets from the Portuguese* is the source of "How do I love thee? Let me count the ways," which is frequently misattributed to Shakespeare.
9. As Dorothy Parker delightfully wrote, "If, with the literate, I am/Impelled to try an epigram;/I never seek to take the credit./We all assume that Oscar said it."

Sound Judgment

July 4th

The soundscape differs on a holiday—
Construction sites fall silent, and the thrum
Of traffic fades beneath the morning gray,[1]
As though the clouds absorb both sound and sun.
But sizzling grills and children's merry shrieks
Will herald hot dog lunches on the grass.
And "Stars and Stripes Forever" seems the peak
Of sweet nostalgia,[2] 'til the warning blast;
O fiery buds exploding into bloom
And strewing golden grains across the sky,
How I adore your sulfurous perfume
As cynical displeasure you defy.
Though I anticipated ringing ears,
I'm pleasantly surprised by joyful tears.[3]

---

1. See "Marine Layer" (January 8th).
2. John Philip Sousa's famous patriotic march, which gets trotted out by every band
and orchestra with an Independence Day concert.
3. It's always a treat when Independence Day occurs during the holiday weekend,
because instead of the usual fireworks that accompany the Symphony pops concerts,
we got to be directly underneath the enormous, city-coordinated fireworks display
over San Diego Bay.

By the Bayside

July 5th

Philosophers and artists of all types
See nature as a source of inspiration;
For seas[1] and roses,[2] stars[3] and tigers' stripes,[4]
Give rise to figurative infatuation.
Still others find the works of human hands—
Cathedrals,[5] tombs,[6] Chicago,[7] Grecian urns,[8]
And broken statues issuing demands[9]—
To be the things for which the spirit yearns.
But, oh, at their divine juxtaposition
Where breezes carry boats across the bay
In midst of outdoor concert's intermission,[10]
As sunset sets the skyline's walls ablaze—
Here I shall find refreshment for my brain
Until I am required to sing again.

1. *Moby Dick; or The Whale* by Herman Melville.
2. "A Red, Red Rose" by Robert Burns.
3. "Choose Something Like a Star" by Robert Frost.
4. "The Tyger" by William Blake.
5. Notre-Dame de Paris (The Hunchback of Notre Dame) by Victor Hugo.
6. "An Arundel Tomb" by Philip Larkin.
7. "Chicago" by Carl Sandburg.
8. "Ode on a Grecian Urn" by John Keats.
9. "Ozymandias" by Percy Bysshe Shelley.
10. Intermission backstage at the San Diego Symphony pops concerts occurs near sunset on San Diego Bay.

Weird Processor

July 6th

When there is just one CD drive on hand
And it's in a PC that's six years old,
To rip the files takes longer than one planned,
And syncing to the cloud takes time untold.
And so to pass the time, I choose to write,
But there's no OpenOffice[1] here, by heaven!
I gnashed my teeth preparing then to fight
With Microsoft and Word 2007.
And yet, my histrionics were unfounded
Since I use Windows programs all the time
For work, so my high dudgeon I have grounded
To focus on my meter and my rhyme.
The only souvenir of software shock[2]
Is seeing that lone file that's labeled .doc.

---

1. Apache OpenOffice, a free word processing program whose updates I generally find to be less disorienting than Microsoft Word's.
2. Word took long enough to update for me to scribble down a good chunk of sonnet.

That Rings a Bowl[1]

July 7th

A dozen singing bowls—which do I want?
The stoneware vessel that makes molars shake?
The painted brass whose sound seems nonchalant?
Is prizing character a grave mistake?
My fingers first alight on red, and since
The bowl agrees to sing for me, the rest
I hardly try, assuming they evince
No notable vibrations in the breast.[2]
But when I have selected it, my hand
Still strays to others, wondering if one
Might speak to me and forcefully demand
That it is mine, that shallow choice undone.
And in the end, I do not fear to choose
The one that dares shake inhibitions loose.

---

1. A writing friend presented all those assembled with a selection of singing bowls
and invited us to choose ones that spoke to us. Singing bowls are bells that are played
inverted (rim upward) either by striking the side with a mallet or by rubbing the rim of
the bowl with the mallet to produce vibrations. They are used in religious ceremonies,
meditation, yoga, therapy, and music.
2. A reference to Oscar Wilde's *The Importance of Being Earnest*, in which
Gwendolyn declares that she wishes to marry a man called Ernest, since the name
produces vibrations and has a music of its own.

Birthday Presence[1]

July 8th

When you spend time with friends but once a year
And you've ostensibly converged to write,
Your first task is to take the time to hear
Each story; reconnect to reunite.
Collectively, we've lost, and we are grieving;
We've made mistakes, wrote things that made us proud,
Annoyed Goliaths—layered interweaving
With one another's lives we are endowed.
And so a gift exchange for birthdays past
Imbues each gift with how that author sees
A most beloved subject in her vast
Complexity and chooses what will please.
And whether it's a notebook or a beer,[2]
These thoughtful tributes shall be held most dear.

---

1. Since the attendees of our writers' retreat gather but once a year (if we're lucky!),
we celebrate everybody's birthdays at once and have a gift exchange.
2. I received local, rare, and seasonal beers that I can't get in California. It was a
brilliant present!

Self Care

July 9th

On such days as one's organs[1] will conspire
Against coherent thought, what can one do
Apart from rest, recover, and retire
And hope the brain will be restored anew?
Indulge in World Cup, perfect omelets,
With stimulating stories interspersed,
Refreshing hot tub soaks with forceful jets,
Accept some days make mediocre verse.
Yet mental scatteredness cannot be faulted
When one is asked for plot, rather than theme,
Fecundity of thought is what's exalted—
Fortuitous requests the self redeem.
At least this day of measly motivation
Occurred when I am taking a vacation.

---

1. It's a cyclical problem, and one that has no feasible cure but time.

Treat Retreat[1]

July 10th

A texted photo of the dogs asleep,
Their legs askew, to laugh in awe and mirth
At strength and balance, sitting in a heap
After I lost my own, upon the earth—
Dramatic readings of e-mails from work,
Absurdly wonderful orchestral fusion,
Receiving day-job queries with a smirk
From someone next to me who's in seclusion.
Professor Hil[2] says writing fiction is
A line direct to joy—a phrase so apt
That perfectly encapsulates the fizz
Of finding an idea that's untapped.
To do so on one's own is quite exciting,
But doing so with dear friends is uniting.

---

1. A paean to the small pleasures of a writers' retreat, from enjoying the company of
those around me to appreciating short messages from home.
2. A member of our writers' group.

Word Sisters

July 11th

One week a year, Eleven Sisters[1] gather
From east and west and far across the sea,
From south and north we come, we who would rather
Abandon lives, though temporarily,
To court sad Melpomene[2] and to laugh
With Thalia,[3] with Polyhymnia[4]
To sing on creativity's behalf,
And hope our homes are blessed by Hestia,[5]
For though we crave this fleeting sacred space
Where words may freely flourish in the brain,
We know we'll leave our leisure in this place,
But acts of our creation will remain.
Collaboratively we hone our craft[6]
In hopes of leaving with a partial draft.

---

1. Sometimes we are fewer or more, but that year we were eleven.
2. Muse of tragedy.
3. Muse of comedy.
4. Muse of sacred poetry, hymn, dance, and eloquence.
5. Goddess of the hearth, home, and family.
6. We were encouraged to work on short stories for an anthology whose theme was gods, goddesses, and demons. It was published the following year as *Immanence* (Story Spring Publishing, 2016).

Idle Theme[1]

July 12th

O daydreams, turn to nightdreams when I sleep,
And let my slumbering mind elect to stay
Enwrapped in luscious pleasure for to steep
Repose in bliss, and keep bad dreams at bay.
For yearning daydreams much prefer to play
While masquerading as reality,
Which makes them lack the sumptuous array
Of one's subconscious mind in reverie.
So take my much belovèd memory
And aspirations for the things to come,
Suffuse them with surprising novelty
To make a whole whose glory strikes me dumb.
In sleep desire, desire then to sleep,
And give to dreaming dreams that I will keep.

---

1. From Puck's epilogue to Shakespeare's *A Midsummer Night's Dream.*

Mischief Laughs

July 13th

I do enjoy the incongruity
Of sitting on a screened-in patio
Surrounded on all sides by broad-leafed trees,
But hearing naught but highway traffic flow;
The lake,1 magnificent and gray, that reaches
Beyond horizon, cool fresh water favors
The weary, yet it's rimmed by private beaches,
Except a tiny strip packed with sunbathers;
When we return, the pool below us beckons,
Our rented home a few stone steps away;
Alas, on solid fence we had not reckoned
That blocks our access. Thank you, HOA.[2]
At least we got some potent interactions
From the frustrations and reduced distractions.

---

1. Lake Michigan, as the retreats tend to be in southwest Michigan.
2. Due to an acrimonious dispute with the owners of the house we rented, the Homeowners Association erected a fence blocking the unit's access to the community's pool. Apparently, a previous party of renters had abused the privilege.

All Good Things[1]

July 14th

Eleven lives, eleven calendars,
Eleven journeys carefully aligned
Eleven minds all eager to confer
And write eleven tales newly assigned.
For seven days eleven sowed the field
With blessed solitude and conversation—
Our House of Our Own[2] then began to yield
The signs of universal germination.
O meadow of ideas in full bloom
Cross-pollinated in lush summertime,
Bear fruits that nourish us when they're consumed
And leaven the eleven in their prime.
Eleven, do not weep that we are scattered;
Improbable convergence is what mattered.

---

1. Written while traveling home from the writers' retreat, also the title of the final
episode of *Star Trek: The Next Generation*.
2. A reference to Virginia Woolf's essay *A Room of One's Own*, which discusses the
basic needs of writers.

Vincible

July 15th

I woke just minutes prior to the alarm
And thought, "That week spent two time zones away
Shall cause me no unpleasantness or harm;
I needn't pussyfoot around today!"
And so I went full-throttle through my tasks
Enthused at solving problems once again
And weighing carefully all questions asked,
Reactivating work parts of my brain.
Adrenaline and quite a bit of luck
Made everything I touched turn into gold,
But afterward, in gear my mind was stuck
And seeking stimulation uncontrolled.
I'm glad my daily sonnet is some surety
Against a false impression of security.[1]

---

1. Though not surety against failing to get to bed at a reasonable hour, alas.

True, Not Free[1]

July 16th

When careful planning and hard work pay off
And dreams seem as if they are coming true,
We sometimes show a tendency to scoff
At how much gratitude good fortune's due;
For in success, self-serving logic lies,
Proclaiming that if something worked for you,
It was because you're virtuous and wise,
And not for things that anyone could do.
Take heed, Triumphant: do not seek to bear
The point of your success, for it can puncture.
Instead, like ancient arch stones, seek to share
Capacity for strength through many junctures.
Renouncing hubris might just put a stop
To waiting for the other shoe to drop.[2]

---

1. Inspired by The Old Globe/Fiasco Theatre production of *Into the Woods*.
2. Cinderella joke that also references the phrase "waiting for the other shoe to drop,"
which means the tension one experiences while waiting for something inevitable to
happen. In New York tenements, it was usual for you to hear your neighbor removing
his shoes, so when you heard one shoe drop and hit the floor, you knew a second
would soon follow.

A Thor-ny Dilemma

July 17th

With sun-warm hammer flush against my palm,
Its haft emblazoned with familiar runes,
I faced the frosted enemy with calm,
And waited for a moment opportune—
And when my comrade pried ajar the door,
I smote the icy ramparts with a cry
My hammer rang with glorious songs of war
As Jotunheim[1] we ventured to defy.
But when the ice was cleared and boxes saved,
The freezer we allowed time to defrost.
Thus, wet linoleum we boldly braved
To bring our doughty tools back to the shop.
A mundane task transformed to something more—
So thank you, Marvel, for your female Thor.[2]

---

1. Home of the Frost Giants in Norse mythology and Marvel's *Thor* comics.
2. In July of 2014, Marvel announced that they would introduce a female Thor. This was, of course, in my mind when I was asked to help open a storage freezer that had frozen shut, especially since the only tool I had on hand was a hammer. I also chose to cosplay her at Comic-Con.

Exploration[1]

July 18th

A ladder leading up to space unknown,
The purview of a neighboring department,
Is hardly barred, but neither is it shown,
Reputed to have been a bum's apartment.
So when I climb and clumsily alight
Upon the slab that leads up to a door,
The roughened pathway fills me with delight—
With eagerness the catwalk I explore.
Alas, the path is short, and leads to naught—
For only hissing pipes lie there beyond,
Within such spaces, enterprise is fraught
With need to see, then sneakily abscond.
Not all adventures end with deeds of glory—
That doesn't mean I don't enjoy the story.

---

1. The older buildings at work can be fun to explore because there is often a less than clear line between public and maintenance spaces.

Encumbered[1]

July 19th

It is a gift to see old things anew,
By virtue of a differing perspective—
Though skeptical initially, I knew
That there was more to it than wit detective.
How sweet to feel an ardor innocent,
Yet aching to be thoroughly expressed
To one particular recipient,
Without him knowing whose joy was professed.
It is enough for me that he's aware
Of widespread adoration from collective,[2]
So when he must contend with the unfair,
I hope that bit of knowledge is protective.
So celebrate another year alive
And know that we take heart to see you thrive.

---

1. A trying-really-hard-not-to-be-creepy sonnet in honor of actor Benedict
Cumberbatch's birthday.
2. One nickname for Cumberbatch fans is the Cumbercollective, which works insofar
as it's not pejorative or insulting and one can joke that it is cumbersome (hee).

Brain Brawn

July 20th

Brain functions are like muscles, in a sense—
Behaviors tone, and frequent exercise
Can make synapses strong and networks dense,
Thanks to plasticity,[1] but this implies
Those mental tasks you rarely will perform,
Enticing challenges or fine intrigue,
May satisfy, but also may transform
Enthusiasm into mind fatigue.[2]
So even when one hums with satisfaction
At one's success in mastering a skill,
A seemingly straightforward daily action
Will feel as if one's trying to ski uphill.
One may prevail with pertinacious fighting,
As I discovered with my daily writing.[3]

---

1. Neuroplasticity is the ability of neurons to adapt to behavioral and environmental changes or damage.
2. It was thought for some time that exercising willpower depletes blood glucose levels in the brain, which leads to irritability, a loss of self-control, and poor decision making.
3. Some sonnets are easier to write than others. This was one of the latter.

The Great Game[1]

July 21st

"Who Would You Rather Kiss?" is quite the game,
Whose rules were passed down from antiquity:[2]
First, one reverses last and Christian name:
So *Black Swan*'s star is Portman Natalie.
Next, two by the creator's names are known
Because with admiration he was rife:
Winona Ryder always is "Win-OWN,"
And Michelle Pfeiffer must be called "Puh-FEIFF."
The final rule[3] is choosing from a pair
Of any your opponents can devise,
Historical celebrities compare—
It's quite a pleasant mental exercise.
Who would you rather kiss: Sinatra Frank,
Or would you go for Williams Junior Hank?

---

1. The nickname given to the rivalry between Britain and Russia for geopolitical power and influence in Central Asia for most of the 19th Century.
2. Or, rather, from the early 1990s, when the game was invented by my friend Tariq and refined by myself and BFF Aliya (see "AAK and EEW," (November 11th)).
3. There are, of course, other optional rules, such as playing with a Scottish accent (rule courtesy Mike).

Fiveplay, an Inflationary Sonnet[1]

July 22nd

Three-night, while walking dogs, my lover spoke
Eleven-derly, he pontific-nine-d
Upon our dachshund, and he made two jokes
That left me laughing and exhilar-nine-d.
And as with b'nine-ted breath my darling w'nine-d,
I offered him whiskered, wee ca-ten.
Three do so as he pleased; we both confl-nine-ed
Our mirth with wit which spurns the asi-ten.
Our kiss beneath one-and-a-quarter moon
Was promise and seduction all at twice.
And so we seized two moments opportune
And had two interludes that were quite nice.
Such two-derful delights within his arms!
I shall commemor-nine his many charms.

---

1. Inflationary Language was invented by comedian Victor Borge. To parody
monetary inflation, he increased numbers hidden in English words by one (e.g.,
"wonderful" becomes "twoderful." His famous example ran: "I ate a tenderloin with
my fork," becomes "I nine an eleven-derloin with my five-k."

Preview[1]

July 23rd

This week will be a week of little sleep,
A week of mad activity and joys
Too numerous to count, which I may keep
For days when all the universe annoys.
This too shall be the week of fervent hope
That few things will adhere to my projections—
With predetermined chaos I will cope,
For tumult and disorder are perfection;
Such gifts of chance are thus to us delivered,
Embraced by those both fortunate and wise.
A plan is but an arrow in a quiver;
Its flight may be predicted or surprise.
Sweet Pandemonium, your aim is true,
Projectile flight's adventure to pursue.

---

1. On Preview Night of San Diego Comic-Con.

Thursday Panels[1]

July 24th

Three hours of keeping watch and five at play,[2]
Analysis, professional enrichment,[3]
Is not an awful way to spend the day,
Despite a slight but lingering disappointment.
It's not that there aren't costumes by the score
That have been built with cleverness and care—
It's not that there aren't awesome panels, for
The guests are frequently beyond compare.
This problem is a privileged one at best;
These hypotheticals for choice events:[4]
Will TV panels help keep me abreast?
Will academic panels be intense?
Like Plato's cave, Hall H[5] contains a show
Of gorgeous shadows we can never know.

---

1. Day One of San Diego Comic-Con.
2. I volunteered for a shift, then met up with a friend for some panels.
3. Comic-Con has incredible professional development panels for creative folks.
4. With so much programming crammed into so few hours, it's a sad inevitability that one can never see everything that one wishes to see.
5. Many of the panels in Hall H feature celebrities and popular media, so the lines for Hall H can be thousands of people long. The hall holds over 6,000 people, but that's only about 5% of all Con attendees. I didn't even try to get in.

Whose Who?

July 25th

A day spent in the company of friends,
Both those of old and those you've now just met,
Upon which everyone overextends
Their energies but cannot be upset,
For each day's crammed with more than one can see
And interstitial loveliness abounds;
Combined nostalgia, wit, and novelty—
Reflected thus in others, it astounds.
Just as it's said that one can't simply walk
To Mordor,[1] nor can one to Ballroom 20,[2]
It's difficult to paraphrase a talk,
When overwhelmed by the delights of plenty.
Our hearts and TARDISes[3] do coincide,
As they're both bigger when you look inside.

1. Paraphrased from Peter Jackson's 2001 film adaptation of J. R. R. Tolkein's *The Lord of the Rings: The Fellowship of the Ring*.
2. Ballroom 20 is the second-largest presentation venue at the convention center and is most frequently used to promote television shows. While the lines are not quite as insane as the Hall H line, you still have to wait in line for a goodly while to get in.
3. The name of the spaceship/time machine in the BBC television series *Doctor Who*, TARDIS stands for Time And Relative Dimension In Space.

Best Episode Ever[1]

July 25th

Sometimes a perfect day is full of stress,
Fatigue and aches, chagrin and too-few meals,
And traffic jams that snarl the streets downtown,
Adrenalin makes weariness surreal,
To see two strangers see and greet each other,
With shibboleths that make the other smile,
And then, embracing, call each other brother—
Such moments do delight as they beguile.
For when unlikely things become the norm,
Preposterous becomes a possibility.
Facilitated frolics can transform
A person suffering from invisibility.
To be amidst a crowd of introverts
Can be a pleasure, even when it hurts.[2]

1. Inspired by Comic Book Guy from *The Simpsons,* whose catchphrase is to declare [thing] the "best/worst [thing] ever."
2. Written for the day I attended Comic-Con dressed as Marvel's recently introduced female Thor and also sang Michael Gioacchino's score for *Star Trek (2009)* with the San Diego Symphony. It was awesome.

The One Stooge[1]

July 27th

Our band contained nine stooges in three rings,
Which was a challenge to coordinate,
Until a new ringmaster had us sing
From music, thus reducing them to eight.[2]
Three more were lost when we changed our PA
To pick up only voices and guitars,[3]
One fled when sets were not in disarray,
Woodshedding charts made two give *au revoir*s.
Which means that set-up doesn't take an hour,
And pieces can improve from week to week,
Mic'ed saxophones no longer overpower,
And set lists are no longer so oblique.
Thus, our stooge count has dwindled down to one,
At least until I say that I am done.[4]

---

1. Reference to the vaudeville/comedy act the Three Stooges.
2. After the disaster on June 29th ("Calibration"), our bandleader made a concerted effort to provide music, or at least roadmaps for the band's charts, to the singers, which was a significant improvement.
3. The bandleader also provided a new microphone set-up, which took less than half the time to set up than the old PA system.
4. Despite significant logistical and musical improvements, I was ready to move on. Especially since I missed the last day of Comic-Con programming to sing that gig.

Con Tiki[1]

July 28th

Four days of fangirl fun at Comic-Con
Will naturally result in lovely things,
From exercising nerdish lexicon
To being filled with awe by costuming.
But in addition to these lovely sights,
And entertaining panels rife with dish,
My own ambitions could not but take flight
In ways that I had never thought to wish.[2]
The concentration of professionals
In industries I hope to penetrate
Outlined how to avert the obstacles,
And list the steps I might concatenate.
Such joy to find an unexpected map
Where waking life and daydream overlap.

---

1. Pun on the *Kon-Tiki*, the raft used by explorer Thor Heyerdahl in 1947 to prove that ancient people could have sailed between South America and Polynesia.
2. I attended a pair of panels on writing for television, something I'd never considered doing before.

Bluffs[1]

July 29th

We are the sum of our experiences,
So having been a lifeguard in my youth
I'm good at seeing past appearances,
Especially when they belie the truth.
So if a lazy parent thinks state law
Does not apply to him or to his brood,[2]
For liability cares not a straw,
And to the pool attendant is quite rude,
When he claims they're lap swimming—clearly guff—
And thinks his word excuses the offenders,
I do not hesitate to call his bluff
And have those kids swim laps 'til they surrender.
Transgression loses charm when it's not fun.
Jerk: 0, Former-Lifeguard Libby: 1.

---

1. A pun on the name of my neighborhood, where the pool mentioned in this sonnet is located, and also a pun on the act of bluffing.
2. Having kids horsing around during lap swim wouldn't bug me so much if we had wave-reducing lane lines, which reduce how often lap swimmers accidentally inhale water. Alas, we do not.

Deferral[1]

July 30th

The circus now has ended, go in peace—
And wait for the inevitable clash
Of life and weariness without surcease
Colloquially known as post-con crash.
How can we fail to mourn collective glee
As for the year it goes into remission,
And fades into the sort of memory
That causes melancholic disposition.
Postponing crash was all that I could do—
By means of sleep and robust exercise.
Of course it's not a thing I can eschew
No matter how I'd wish it otherwise.
Alas, we all must pay this bitter price
For having tasted part of paradise.

---

1. Returning to the daily grind after going wild at Comic-Con is challenging.

Finishing Down

July 31st

It is exquisite torture to succumb
To the desire to rest upon the bed
While finding heavy eyelids bothersome,
As lower droops the hebetudinous head.
But even as the lids rejoice to meet,
The brain cries out that tasks remain undone,
Thus jerking you awake—"Did I complete
A sonnet? Could I post an old re-run?"
But no, I grit my teeth and soldier on
Despite the fact my memory's a sieve,
And my ideas die before they spawn
A single thing resembling narrative.
But when it's done my mind and body race
To be the first to Morpheus's embrace.[1]

---

1. Often when I write a sonnet, the couplet is the last thing I write. However, this couplet arrived at the same time I came up with this idea (I rejected a couple of others first), which gave me something to write towards.

August

Handfast Friends[1]

August 1st

Today, two individuals were joined,
Four siblings, eight immediate relations,
And over sixteen other friends enjoined
To give support and joy to celebrations—
For love of one another two were wed,
For love of two, so many came together
To give good wishes for their road ahead;
That it be strewn with great things altogether.
Therefore, it is no wonder that among
Those gathered were the seeds of friendships new,
That when the vows were vowed and songs were sung
Affinities unfurled and old ones grew.
This gathering was notably inclined
To have respect for all the ties that bind.

---

1. A sonnet written in celebration of my friends' wedding. Congratulations, Ellie and Laura!

Inclemency[1]

August 2nd

A summer in the midst of coastal scrub
Is not a normal time or place for rain,
As evidenced by copiousness of shrubs:
That's all our meager rainfall can sustain.
And so an August barbecue would seem
To be a suitable, in-season thing,
So much so that no-one would ever dream
That climate might preclude the reveling.
Surprise! Unseasonable humidity
And low gray clouds composed of more than mist
Required of plans distinct fluidity,
Until a lightning strike that barely missed.
While weather wreaked impressive disarray,
At least it wasn't on the wedding day.

---

1. Thankfully the cold rain didn't arrive on my friends' wedding day, but it did put a damper on the celebratory bonfire planned for the next day.

Luxury of Laps[1]

August 3rd

One swim revealed that I was out of shape.
The second showed it's easy to improve.
The third time out I managed to escape
With only broken goggles—I could move!
And on the fourth, new goggles now procured,
I managed to complete my old workout,
Though celebration would be premature,
As tempting as it is to whoop and shout.
It's really not impressive to have done
A thing my body trained to do for years.
Though I confess, I find it rather fun
To feel familiar strokes slip into gear.
I savor my accomplishments but know
That I have quite a distance yet to go.[2]

---

1. Being a person who swam competitively in her youth, it's disheartening to feel out of shape.
2. This statement was a bit funny because this sonnet marked the first time I saved the sonnet on my blog on the day it was written, but I failed to hit the big blue "Publish" button. I didn't notice it was missing until August 8th, at which point I posted it with a chagrined note of apology. At least the subject of the sonnet gives me the excuse of having had a waterlogged brain.

Mind the Gap[1]

August 4th

Sometimes I wish my brain came with a switch
Designed to lessen mental disarray
By flipping all my thoughts without a hitch
Between transcendence and the everyday.
Thus, in the midst of requisite routine
To wandering daydreams I would be immune,
And while creating, I'd remain serene
Untroubled by concerns most picayune.
And yet, I'd fear to conquer by divide,
Since great plans sometimes come from thoughts amok—
Attempts to segregate my mental sides
Might leave me lost if switches ever stuck.
One doesn't need to go to drastic lengths
To quash an inconvenience that's a strength.

---

1. A pun on the warning issued to UK rail passengers boarding and disembarking trains that also questions whether or not I mind having different mental settings and if it's a bad thing to have to switch between them.

Score[1]

August 5th

Wherever I go, music follows me,
Accompanying everything I do.
It demonstrates persistent industry,
Enticing me to sing at every cue.[2]
Some other folks have soundtracks of their own,
Observable in how they move through spaces.
And one can never truly be alone
When yours with someone's music interlaces.
Of course, not everyone on earth can hear
Or thinks such sounds can be a joy to make;
Our sensibilities may yet cohere
Through music loud enough to make walls shake.
So own that composition life provides
And moments when with others it collides.

---

1. Inspired by an Arcade Fire concert, as part of their *Reflektor* tour.
2. Thankfully, my colleagues don't seem to mind me adding accompaniment to my
workdays.

Fancy Plants

August 6th

Magnolia, crowned with pearly blossoms, stands
With silvered boughs aloft in shapely poses,
Enameled leaves like shining emerald hands,
The luminous flowers' scent delights all noses—
A striking scion of an ancient race,[1]
Whose forebears predate bees for pollination,[2]
Arboreal epitome of grace,
And source of taxonomic irritation.[3]
But when leaves brown and fall upon the ground,
Their work of photosynthesis will shift
To mischief and creating startling sounds;
Crack underfoot, and clattering adrift.
Though lovely they may be, it is preferred
To love them for their sense of the absurd.

---

1. Fossils of plants of the family Magnoliacaeae have been dated at 95 million years old.
2. It's been theorized that since the trees predate bees, ancient magnolias were pollinated by beetles.
3. Because the family is so ancient and survived many major geological events, taxonomists had great difficulty charting how species of magnolia were related until DNA sequencing became available.

Jargon Infarctions[1]

August 7th

When one constructs a mystery or thriller,
Recondite research must be done, because
It's not enough to know who is the killer,
The reader must believe in what he does.
When injuries occur, make sure you know
If death could follow; if so, why and when.
Or ask a black ops soldier, who can show
You how to kill a person with a pen.
So don't mistake concussion for contusion,
Ablation for abrasion, reflux-reflex,
Or arthroscope and orthoscope—confusion
Results when words are not what one expects.
Your book will have a rather grim prognosis
If you mistake necrosis for neurosis.

---

1. I shared my notes from a mystery/thriller writers' panel at Comic-Con called *101 Ways to Kill a Man* with my friend Melissa. A story about the perils of medical jargon inspired the medical malapropism in the title and the sonnet that follows.

Watching the Watchers[1]

August 8th

With house lights up, arena stages let
The audience, once settled and in place,
See not just every facet of the set,
But also every audience member's face.
And with a mustache or a lock of hair,
The seemingly familiar will beguile
And lead one to consider and to stare—
Is that someone I know? And should I smile?
And does the very nature of the space,
In which performers don identities
Like costumes, make it easy to replace
Unknown with known to ease one's vague unease?
At least it's possible to take some pride
In friendly faces you've identified.

---

1. Inspired by spotting my friend Amelia sitting on the opposite side of the arena stage
at the Old Globe's production of Ronald Harwood's *Quartet*.

Full of Noises[1]

August 9th

Past midnight on a muggy August night,
All ceiling fans turned high, doors open wide,
The full moon bathing all in silver light,
A silent dog and owner pass outside—
But my dogs fear that dog a mortal threat
And with their barking house and home defend
Five seconds later, they've cause to regret—
They're shushed and banished, yet the noise portends
Retaliation from the batty neighbor,
Whose tolerance of dogs is low-to-none,
Which comes in air horn blast,[2] a rattled saber,
But even she has yet to be outdone.
She cannot blame her canine neighbors for
The jet that passes over with a roar.

---

1. From Shakespeare's *The Tempest,* act 3, scene 2.
2. One of my neighbors took to policing nearby dogs and their owners by blasting an
air horn out the window if she could hear a dog barking, regardless of the time,
duration of the barking, or other circumstances. This was about as effective as you'd
think (i.e., not at all), but clearly it made her feel better.

In the Soup

August 10th

The sign read "Wanton Soup," clearly misspelled,
Inviting one for dumplings served in broth.
I must confess my appetite was quelled
Imagining the culinary froth
That would be violent soup, like cruelty,
Assembled with malicious unconcern,
Or lewd and lawless soup whose novelty
Entices all to taste and end up burned.
And yet such soup could be luxurious,
So fine of texture, sumptuous of taste,
That first bite could be something glorious—
Perhaps my trepidation was misplaced.
For wanton's a delicious word, I know;
Perhaps I'd find the soup equally so.[1]

---

1. Alas, I shall never know how wanton the soup was, as I was really in the mood for ramen ("Beautiful, Beautiful Soup!" January 22nd).

Fair Robin I Love[1]

August 11th

Salacious language, sex, and Nick at Nite—
Such things were unavailable, forbidden.
Within those boundaries, naught felt as right
As what I somehow sensed was barely hidden;
Beneath those PG ratings lurked a power,
Both unrepentant and so full of glee,
That loudly, quickly, joyfully devoured
The boundaries of what I was to be.
For here was cleverness with heart and mind,
Refreshing frankness, virtuosic skill,
Performances whose eras they defined,
And earning their creator much good will.[2]
That shared highs brought lone lows seems cruelty—
This great dead poet[3] will live on in me.

---

1. *In memoriam* Robin Williams, the title is taken from an aria from Kirke Mechem's opera *Tartuffe,* which is based on Molière's play of the same name.
2. Pun on the film *Good Will Hunting*. Williams's performance in the film won him an Academy Award for Best Supporting Actor.
3. Peter Wier's film *Dead Poets Society,* in which Robin Williams starred, was a particular boon to this bookish eleven-year-old.

*ucking Sonnet[1]

August 12th

A lexeme nonpareil, though one that's stuck
With so much baggage there's a yen to chuck
It out with more archaic words. So cluck
Your tongue no more: it has been struck,
From my vocabulary, I shall buck
The trend to use profanity amok,
As if in time I had become unstuck—
And so it goes,[2] with bravery and pluck.
But oh, to do without: am I a schmuck
Who arbitrarily discards a shuck
That might prove valuable? I have been struck
With crippling doubt, though I'm an honest Puck.[3]
Perhaps no-one will notice what I've snuck
In by omission, with a bit of luck.

1. This might have been titled "An Extremely Juvenile Sonnet," but that was already taken (April 14th). When I was in high school, several friends and I founded a club known as the PRF for the preservation and appreciation of the f-word. This is also another sonnet featuring a single end rhyme throughout, as in "Straight A's" (March 24th).
2. References to Kurt Vonnegut's *Slaughterhouse Five*.
3. From Puck's final speech in Shakespeare's *A Midsummer Night's Dream.*

Protean Valentine[1]

August 13th

Two gentlemen made fools by love: the first
As changeful as the sea, the other staid,
Whilst constant lovers undergo the worst—
Abandoned, traded, badly-used, betrayed.
It seems a diatribe denouncing love,
How courtliness goes easily astray,
Deserting chivalry, the lack thereof
Turns love to thief and page to fiancée.
And yet, amidst the faithless and the fooled,
Just one would face disgrace and great commotion
Because by selflessness his heart is ruled,
A singular example of devotion.
That's why my favorite lines of dialogue
Are spoken by a fool about his dog.[2]

---

1. Inspired by the Old Globe's production of Shakespeare's *Two Gentlemen of Verona*.
The play is near and dear to my heart, as it's the first Shakespeare play I ever saw live,
many years ago at (you guessed it!) integrated arts camp.
2. The fool, Launce, first berates his dog as heartless for failing to shed tears. In spite
of this, he later takes a beating for his dog's misbehavior, which is by far the most
selfless act of love in the whole play and stands in stark (but funny) contrast to the
central romances.

On My Dog, Whose Needs Are Urgent[1]

August 14th

O hound whose evening walk was rather early,
Expending patience will cause you no harm.
Your bark can't signal what I think now, surely——
It's still ten minutes prior to my alarm.
But as I lie, you come not to my side,
Nor wag and frolic by me when I rise.
Your sleepy stretch and kisses I'm denied,
I pray this lack no accident implies.
No yard have I where you may find relief
Nor doggy door by which you may egress.
For in your brawny bladder I've belief,
But feel a twinge of guilt at your distress.
Your happy mien tells me your sorrow died
The moment that you found a tree outside.

---

1. I suspect that many dog owners recognize this nexus of guilt and exhaustion.

Thine Own Self[1]

August 15th

Immortal love to stand the test of time,
A noble heart enslaved by jealousy,
A shining soul draws villains to a crime—
Cathartic Tragedy is just not me.
Usurpers, bastards, questions of succession,
Assassinations, infidelity,
Great speeches, battles, learning painful lessons—
I'm positive that I'm no History.
Parades of gods, foul acts demand redemption,
Bucolic themes without mud, dung, or fleas,
Since reunited loves merit exemption—
Am I a Problem Play? A Romance? Please.
To human weakness grudgingly concede—
And laugh, for I'm a Comedy, indeed.

---

1. From Polonius's speech in *Hamlet,* act 1, scene 3.

238

String Theory[1]

August 16th

One hand has but five fingers, yet guitars
Are strung with six strings in the standard tuning,
The intervals aren't constant, and the barres
Are difficult at first fret; when you're crooning
Your poor guitar must rest upon your knee,
Which ruins voice support at times you play,
Unless the need for strap you did foresee,
While fingertips by steel are stripped away.
But if you learn four chords, you hold the key
To rock and tens of thousands other songs
John Denver, Green Day, U2, "Let it Be"—
It makes one tolerant of seeming wrongs.
To paraphrase an understanding teacher,
It's not a bug—it's just a charming feature.

---

1. Thoughts from practicing guitar. Something I ought to do more often.

239

Trollolol[1]

August 17th

Norwegian trolls are apt to live in caves
Unmotivated to assist the lost
Who might escape through terribly close shaves,
Though possibly at quite a heavy cost.
Trolls on the internet make enemies
Of those displaying joy and earnestness.
They're loath to pass up opportunities
To revel in intemperate address.
And yet the latter troll is aptly named,
Because they do not share the core belief
That content's not created to be flamed—
Their joy is turning earnestness to grief.
It's tempting to dismiss them as a whole,
But one can't tell the monsters from the trolls.[2]

---

1. Refers to a popular video of baritone Eduard Anatolyevich Khil singing a Russian
song in 1976 with nonsense lyrics "tro lo lo lo lo," which was often used to respond to
people suspected of internet trolling (i.e., deliberately trying to provoke others
through the use of inflammatory rhetoric).
2. Inspired by the virulent harassment and doxxing of female game developers and
media critics during the GamerGate controversy, which started when an ex-boyfriend
of game developer Zoë Quinn incited members of online forums to attack her by
making spurious claims that she slept with a video game journalist in exchange for
positive reviews of a game she developed.

The Bucket List[1]

August 18th

To raise awareness for a dread disease,
A challenge to pour ice upon one's head
(Though just enough to shock and not to freeze)
And post an online video, has spread.
Now social media are inundated
With people getting in on all the fun.
By seeing others, we're manipulated—
What is this? Eighties *Nickelodeon*?[2]
Though I am tempted just to roll my eyes
Each time another bucket is upended,
I think it rather churlish to chastise:
A gimmick raising millions is quite splendid.
And when the world is battered by unrest,[3]
It's nice to be distracted by wet chests.

---

1. The Ice Bucket Challenge was a campaign to raise awareness for ALS (amyotrophic lateral sclerosis, also known as Lou Gherig's disease), in which a person could either donate to the ALS Association or pour a bucket of ice water on their heads, then challenge others to do the same (many donated as well as posted videos). The campaign went viral, and movie stars, professional athletes, philanthropists, musicians, politicians, and even fictional characters got in on the fad.
2. Refers to the Canadian sketch comedy show *You Can't Do That on Television,* in which uttering certain words of phrases could get a cast member doused with water or green slime.
3. See "Ferguson," August 19th.

Ferguson[1]

August 19th

I wish that there was something I could say
To staunch this wound that's bled for ten days now.
Though I'm no doctor, treatments underway
Are ones the reasonable would disallow.
So as we watch in horror as the body
Deteriorates with every antidote,
We realize the remedy is shoddy
And loudly question any who promote
This course of physic—it can never heal;
It cannot help the young unjustly dead;
It will not ease the family's ordeal,
It won't address injustices widespread.
There's nothing I can do, this I admit,
And nothing to say, but I'm saying it.[2]

1. On August 9th, 2014, an unarmed teen, Michael Brown, was fatally shot by police in Ferguson, Missouri. The murky circumstances of the shooting ignited protests and riots, and prompted national discussion of violent policing and the way it disproportionately targets minorities.
2. Refers to John Cage's *Lecture on Nothing.*

A Sort of Runic Rhyme[1]

August 20th

For three long nights refurbished bells have rung,
To gather in the teeming congregation.
Enchanting melodies the choir has sung
Above the thrilling tintinnabulation.
In nineteen ninety-six these bells first tolled,[2]
And then again in nineteen ninety-nine,[3]
Though they were cast from a Parisian mold,[4]
They spent a dozen years in redesign.[5]
We postulants[6] shall toil these lengthy days
That we might justify the keen promotion
And faith in our spectacular display
Of faith and hope and personal devotion.
If these first nights may serve as a predictor,
Celestial spoils are due unto the Victor.[7]

---

1. From Edgar Alan Poe's "The Bells."
2. Disney's musical animated film *The Hunchback of Notre Dame* was released in 1996.
3. *Der Glöckner von Notre Dame*, a stage musical based on the animated film, premiered in Germany in 1999 and ran for three years.
4. The original source of both film and musical was Victor Hugo's 1831 novel *Notre-Dame de Paris (The Hunchback of Notre Dame)*.
5. Disney Theatrical produced the US premiere of the revised stage musical at La Jolla Playhouse (and later, the Paper Mill Theatre).
6. The onstage chorus, who began rehearsing in August, wore monk's robes for all performances.
7. A pun on Victor Hugo.

Ultimate

August 21st

The Rule of Malheur 12[1] is simply this:
It can't be ordered as your final beer,
And if this aphorism you dismiss,
More Malheur 12 is destined to appear.
So if one buys a bottle for the table
The people who procure successive rounds
Consult the bottle list and are not able
To find beer more loved or more renowned.
Thus, when a party's late to join the crowd,
And everyone has reached beer saturation,
Someone who asks what beer will leave us wowed
Will send a bottle in appreciation.
The Rule may seem a brag[2] and not a warning,
But you will understand it in the morning.

---

1. Malheur 12 is a 12% ABV quadruple style beer brewed by Brouwerij De
Landtsheer in Buggenhout, Belgium. It is sweet, delicious, and dangerous.
2. A humblebrag, as seen in "I Envy You, Getting to Watch the Show" (May 21st).

244

Acceptance

August 22nd

The wait between audition[1] and result
Could drive less sanguine people to distraction,
For even if one does well, to exult
Is premature, since knowing just a fraction
Of others seeking placement and their skill
Leaves many variables yet undefined.
Though premature analysis may thrill,
It won't affect what parts will be assigned.
Acceptance, when it comes, is pure relief
And pleasure that your wish has been fulfilled,
That's followed by dismay and disbelief
For those whose choral voices have been stilled.
The time for singing will come soon enough—
For now, I sympathize with the rebuffed.

---

1. This round of biennial auditions for returning choir members resulted in some significant personnel changes. I'm very glad I sang an aria with high notes in it.

Call and Response[1]

August 23rd

When music joyfully calls out to us,
It takes a moment for us to perceive
The invitation to respond, and thus
We pause, not wishing to appear naïve.
But with the second call we understand
Just what we are expected to repeat.
It's both request and cheerful reprimand
That silence makes the music incomplete.
To ask an audience to join the song
Turns passive listener to chorus member.
The phrases are not intricate or long,
And with each repetition, they remember.
So raise your arms and voices when you're told—
Your pleasure will increase a hundredfold.

---

1. On being encouraged to sing along at a Trombone Shorty concert.

A Deep Breath[1]

August 24th

To breathlessly anticipate new faces
And tales carved out from layers of history
With playfulness in interstitial spaces
While solving a dramatic mystery,
But then receive a quite familiar setting,
Recurring characters, plot lines, and tropes,
Proportion issues that could use some vetting——
Was it constructed just to dash my hopes?
What cynic put such petty thoughts inside
The women's heads and had them fight in leather,
Thus stopping them from walking alongside
The hero? I hope this is no bellwether.
Yet, I enjoyed this Doctor's first appearance
And sit in hope of much improved coherence.

---

1. Refers to "Deep Breath," the *Doctor Who* series 8 premiere, which was the first
episode to star Peter Capaldi as the thirteenth Doctor.

Ad Lib[1]

August 25th

Through force of Will[2] came sonnets into being,
Deliberately chosen as a form
Requiring glibness, and perhaps foreseeing
The poem's liberation from the norm—
Instead of celibate and mannered verse,
That rarely touches on libidinous matter,
These sonnets are both liberal and perverse;
A library of flippancy and smatter.
Like Caliban on Sycorax's isle,[3]
I take great liberties to claim descendence,
With quodlibets,[4] the mantle of Will's style,
Though fallible to pride and lacking essence.
My caliber's discernible through bluster
Within this seeming endless filibuster.

---

1. *Ad libitum*, to speak without preparation. Also a Latin pun on my name meaning "To (or for) Lib(by)."
2. Pun on William Shakespeare's name.
3. A reference to the monster Caliban from Shakespeare's *The Tempest*.
4. A matter of philosophical debate, and, alternately, a fun medley of popular tunes. Plus there's another "lib" in it!

The Yoke Is Easy[1]

August 26th

As one who walks two dogs when one dog balks
And lags behind to seek enticing scents,
The other pulling forward as she stalks
Her feline quarry, such is the suspense
Of living with one firm foot on the earth,
Accepting obligations of that life,
Though dull, because one understands the worth
Of duty when it minimizes strife—
But at such times the striving soul will see
Those who have made a living at their dreams
And disregard pernicious jealousy
Which whispers that it's perfect as it seems.
To know no life's protected from despair
Makes compromises easier to bear.

---

1. Refers to the chorus "His Yoke Is Easy" from G. F. Handel's *Messiah,* text from Matthew 11:30.

On Villanelles, or, No Villanelles

August 27th

It was suggested that my daily sonnet
Is insufficient challenge—I should spread
My wings and place a feather in my bonnet
By writing daily villanelles instead.
The form demands two oft-repeated rhymes
To end five three-line stanzas, two refrains,
Each one of which repeated several times,
And finally resolved with a quatrain.
To write just five more lines in every day
Might seem a fairly trivial expansion,
But repetitious forms bring me dismay,
As well as fewer rhymes and muddled scansion.
While villanelles enjoy some notoriety,[1]
I much prefer the fourteen-line variety.

---

1. The band They Might Be Giants performs a song called "Hate the Villanelle," which includes the lyrics, "With these picky rules and odd jigsaw rhymes/Curses, these verses are my prison cell." Naturally, the lyrics are a villanelle.

Do You Want to Write a Sonnet?[1]

August 28th

As every English student has found out,
A sonnet can be writ by anyone—
From rhyming word pairs inspiration sprouts,
Resulting in a bit of scansion fun,
And pride in saying, "Look at what I wrote!"
Enjoy your kinship with great wordsmiths past,
Since, thanks to Shakespeare, sonnet form connotes
Refinement, passion, cleverness, and class.
Now, since you know the basics of the craft,
And your successes cannot but impel
You onward, you are competent to draft
Sestina,[2] ballad,[3] ode,[4] or villanelle.[5]
Don't be intimidated. Sit. Think. Write.
It's pretty much what I do every night.

---

1. I finally got around to watching the Disney film *Frozen* and appreciated the catchy tunes. This sonnet's title is inspired by "Do You Want to Build a Snowman?"
2. A thirty-nine-line verse form that repeats the end-words of each line in every six-line stanza in strict rotation, culminating in an "envoi" of three lines. One example is Ezra Pound's "Altaforte."
3. A plot-driven poem that alternates four and three-foot lines, like Samuel Taylor Coleridge's *Rime of the Ancient Mariner.*
4. A metered, rhyming stanza in praise of someone or something, such as John Keats's "Ode to a Nightingale".
5. See "On Villanelles, or No Villanelles" (August 27th) or Dylan Thomas's famous villanelle, "Do not go gentle into that good night."

251

Something Like a Star[1]

August 29th

The beauty of a star is best admired
Through distillation of the atmosphere,
So purest light may grateful eyes inspire
When it in darkened firmament appears.
Though from a distance it may seem perfection
A star might crush you with its gravity,
In shadow starve you with its pale reflection,
Or burn you with its light's intensity.
Scorn not your perfect orbit of the sun
Whose brightness feeds your body, mind, and soul.
Though seasons pass as revolutions run
Its warmth and light all weary hearts console.
Remember: when regarded from afar
Your sun is someone else's distant star.

---

1. From Robert Frost's "Choose Something Like a Star."

Two-Ton Golden Retriever[1]

August 30th

Though Ogden Nash described you "homely beast"
And intimated you're preposterous
I do not find you either in the least,
You lovely single-horned rhinoceros.
So fond of praise and petting, you endure
With your prehensile upper lip high fives
By which sweet turnip slices you procure,
Though they are not essential to survive.
Yet thanks to those who think your horn is magic
Though it's composed of only keratin,
Which makes up hair and fingernails, it's tragic;
Your numbers dwindle, to the world's chagrin.[2]
With untold gratitude do I behold
Your ears when sunshine turns their fringes gold.

---

1. I asked for and received a backstage tour at the San Diego Zoo for my birthday, where I got to meet many wonderful animals, including a one-horned rhino, whose keeper referred to his friendly, personable charge as a two-ton golden retriever.
2. Geopolitics are complicated, but the fact that rhinoceros horns have no unique medicinal properties is simple and beyond dispute.

Creative Process[1]

August 31st

Step one: think. Step two: write ideas down.
Step three: outline. Analysis: step four.
Step five: get feedback. Step six: shop around
For expert comments. Seven: ask for more.
And eight: forget or publish or submit.
That's it. That's really all you have to do
Unless it's deemed your efforts are unfit,
Necessitating scrupulous review.
But if you read and find that what you wrote
Is truth—precisely what you wished to say;
Consider: cleverness it may denote;
Its zenith may be reached another day.
Time and fecundity are panaceas—
So spend your time encouraging ideas.[2]

---

1. My creative process, anyway.
2. And for goodness's sake, write them down!

September

Tensile Strength

September 1st

As burdens that begin as bearable
Then painfully dig into tender flesh,
So stress can go from fine to terrible
When in the cycle one becomes enmeshed—
As picayune regrets become hot shame,
Unfinished projects build up, unsurmounted.
Inconsequential failures focus blame,
And with perverse precision they're recounted.
Resistance comes through suitable distraction,
By stimulation of that perfect space
Within the brain that spurs it into action—
Familiar motions harmful thoughts replace.
When smothered by the ash of desperation,
Seek comfort in the fire of your creation.[1]

---

1. Writing this sonnet was an act of self-preservation. I figured if I could keep doing the sonnet project, I could dig myself out of any hole. Thankfully, I managed to do both.

Periodicity

September 2nd

It is an unaccountable relief
To realize your feelings of ennui,
Which you had first attributed to grief,
Comes from a cause more elementary.[1]
Death anniversaries must needs recur,[2]
But while they may engender melancholy,
With passing time they cause less of a stir,
So blaming them for fretfulness is folly.
To pinpoint the determinant does not
Make one's frustration easy to conceal,
And yet one can take comfort in the thought
That they're not caused by anything that's real.
I've every expectation this malaise
Will not endure past five to seven days.

---

1. See "Self Care" (July 9th).
2. See "Argument Clinic" (June 24th).

No Thanks[1]

September 3rd

A fad of gratitude has spread throughout
My social media,[2] and challenged all
Who read those thanks to do the same. I doubt
That every thanker has the wherewithal
To name three things they're thankful for each day
For thirty days. I'm loath to loathe the thought
Of people taking time to think and say
"Thank you!" but it's too easily forgot—
It takes a certain type of proud obsessive
To do a long-term project of that kind,
And it can be decidedly oppressive
To always have the project in your mind.[3]
And yet, like writing sonnets, gratitude
Brings mindfulness and betters attitude.[4]

---

1. Continuation of the previous day's malaise, but with bonus curmudgeonliness.
2. The "Thirty Day Gratitude Challenge" encouraged participants to list something for which they are grateful once a day for thirty days.
3. Nine months into the sonnet project, I was all too familiar with the project's downside.
4. The upside of the sonnet project.

Counted Sweetest[1]

September 4th

The football season kickoff was tonight,
Which spelled the end of those fantastic days
In which I wore the golden crown outright,
My badge of victory. How fortune plays
Desire! I, who had finished in last place
So many times before, should then succeed—
The joker suddenly became the ace,
And found herself reluctant to concede.
Though many weeks shall pass before it's known
Who's next up in our league's line of succession,
Each point's an increment that makes the throne
More out of reach in this, my lame duck session.
And yet, if I'm to lose, I'll double down.
Quixotic grows the head that wore the crown.[2]

---

1. Title from Emily Dickinson's "Success is counted sweetest," and refers to actually winning one of my fantasy football leagues.
2. A play on a line from act 3, scene 1 of Shakespeare's *Henry IV, Part II*, "Uneasy lies the head that wears a crown."

Sonnet for Prepared Poet[1]

September 5th

[Oh] why in heaven's name don't people read?
A fugue is a more complicated game.
Art goes within and I don't see the need—
It was a pleasure and now just the same.
Do you live or do you insist on words?
Consider this non-dualistically:
Accepted [I] major and minor thirds;
[And] This is pleasing momentarily.
This sonnet has been thus composed of lines
From lectures, poems, and writings by John Cage.[2]
A phrase, like sound, can be thus redefined
When juxtaposed or heard upon a stage.
Of that great polymath, it's but a facet—
And admiration for him should be [tacet].[3]

---

1. In honor of John Cage's birthday, the title plays on Cage's *Sonatas and Interludes for Prepared Piano*.
2. Specifically, History of Experimental Music in the United States, Eric Satie, 45' For a Speaker, and Silence.
3. Pun on tacit, which means unspoken but understood, and tacet, a score marking indicating silence, which refers to Cage's famous composition *4'33"*, which comprises three tacet movements that total four minutes and thirty-three seconds of performed silence.

Tycho Brahe's Pet Moose[1]

September 6th

The beauty of the internet is this:
All things connected via hyperlinks.
That simple queries stand at the abyss
Of boundless knowledge and unplanned high jinx.
Perform a search on Henry Purcell's life,
And one may find the name of his librettist,[2]
Who translated a poem that was rife
With medicine and named dread syphilis.[3]
And thus inspired, I reached out to a friend
With whom I had spontaneously composed
A suite upon that ailment.[4] Hitting "send,"
The tyranny of distance was deposed.
All ignorance belies, knowledge acquits—
All one need do is simply search for it.

---

1. Many years ago, I wrote a blog entry about receiving someone else's card with a bouquet that referred to The Great Moose of Texas, which led to my friend Jeff writing a ballad about the Great Moose of Texas and my friend Andrew referring to Tycho Brahe's pet moose, to the amusement and edification of everybody who read the post.
2. Nahum Tate, who did the libretto for Purcell's opera *Dido and Aeneas,* was also England's poet laureate.
3. Tate translated Girolamo Fracastoro's poem *Syphilis sive Morbus Gallicus* into heroic couplets.
4. Eric and I called it "Syphilis: A Tone Poem in Four Stages."

Fortune Favors

September 7th

When heat demands escape by any means
The beach would seem a perfect place to turn,
Where ocean breezes cool the space between
The savage sun and water; to discern
If such a trip is wise takes too much time,
And, moment seized, we brave the crowds and sand
To find not only are conditions prime,
They could not be more perfect if we'd planned.
The lowest tide: broad flat like antique mirror,
Whose storm-fed swells roll arcs of water shoreward,
Enticing timid beasties¹ to come nearer—
Despite increasing depth, they venture forward.
From joyful play they all too quickly tire,
And somehow sunburned shoulders I acquire.

---

1. Ocean Beach's Dog Beach is one of our favorite waterside dog parks.

Training Wheels

September 8th

It's nice, when one is training employees,[1]
When complications with a plain solution
Arise in those precise technologies
That I know intimately. Resolution
May seem impressive, and when reproduced
Assume the awesome aspect of amazing:
Phenomena invoking the abstruse,
And improvising masterworks of phrasing.
But ultimately, I expect no thanks
For helping someone master competence—
For no-one's ignorance is truly blank,
And having me to train brings no expense.
For now, I will enjoy the adulation
For paltry feats of prestidigitation.

---

1. Training new colleagues is one of the more fun parts of my job. I've made just about every mistake possible, so I'm usually able to help.

Goodbye, Chuck[1]

September 9th

At first, was a case of touchiness
Which oftentimes suggests that I am tired,
But gradually awareness coalesced
That something was amiss with my insides.[2]
It then became a trial of withstanding
Until I reached a place of privacy
And waiting, shivering for understanding
Of all my symptoms alimentary.
And after hours of curling in a ball,
At last, the illness's apotheosis
Came over me, and I was rid of all
That stood between me and a good prognosis.
The shaking ceased and all was calm at last,
I dearly hope the worst of this is past.

---

1. Food poisoning struck after a meeting I attended. The meeting would have been an excellent subject for a sonnet, but my mind was on other things by the time I got around to writing.
2. Apparently, the illness also impeded my ability to rhyme precisely.

Sea Legs[1]

September 10th

When one's been buffeted by fickle waves
And left so weak it's difficult to stand,
Those tentative first steps will be what saves
You from the blandishments of solid land.
For while it may seem safest to avert
Approaching gales by lingering on shore,
Contentment may be found by the inert,
But joy is found by giving trust once more.
So hold fast to your crewmates and your ship;
For all of us by storms are rocked and blown,
And even the meticulous can slip.
There is no prize for doing it alone.
So think no more about what might have been—
And work to get your sea legs back again.

---

1. An extended metaphor for recovering from food poisoning and not being at liberty
to take a sick day.

The Watched Pot

September 11th

I watched a pot of soup until it boiled
To thumb my nose at that old aphorism
And see each gently swirling bead of oil
Refract the working light like tiny prism.
While flakes of parsley circulate below
The tranquil surface, wispy ghosts of steam
Disperse, as bubbles grow and burst, but no,
It only simmers, boiling though it seems.
Though heat and smell were pleasant, I confess,
I saw no beauty in that bile-hued pot.
It boiled at last—in that there was success—
But all I gained was canned soup, piping hot.[1]
It's good that soup was all I sought, no more,
Since in that time the Steelers[2] failed to score.

---

1. Apparently, I had recovered enough from food poisoning to know that inexpensive canned soup is probably not going to taste particularly good.
2. You know it's an unexciting football game when you prefer to watch soup boil.

A Spoonful of Sugar[1]

September 12th

A drink of water didn't do the trick,
Nor *hic* did holding breath and swallowing,
And scaring me won't happen, trust me. *hic*
Instead, *hic* I'm self-pity-wallowing.
I'll suck *hic* lemon, breathe into a bag,
Though by these remedies I can't be cured—
I can't go back a meal and this time lag,
So to these tiresome tics I'm *hic* inured.
And yet, declining "this"[2] in ancient tongue
Entices me to truly go for broke
Ensuring classics scholars I'm among
When I make puns involving *hic* haec hoc.3
The vagus nerve[4] is hard *hic* to appease,
So why not make whatever jokes you please?

---

1. A spoonful of sugar, as Mary Poppins sang, may help the medicine go down, but it's also long been used as a hiccup remedy.
2. In Latin, "this" is "hic," and declining demonstrative pronouns begins "hic haec hoc."
3. I make this joke every time I get the hiccups. It's also quite fun to say "huius huius huius."
4. Cranial nerve responsible for the heart, digestive tract, and hiccups.

Name That Tune

September 13th

Once, fifteen years ago, I heard a tale
Of how a classic song had been conceived,[1]
Which sprang to mind today in some detail,
While bits of music I sought to retrieve.
For as I pondered how tunes are constructed,
And sang the ones that I thought found success,
A novel one appeared quite unobstructed
By thoughts I had the good sense to suppress.
But having written down in messy hand
The notes, the tune, though crude, can now live on,
The vagaries of memory withstand,
And new ideas for other ditties spawn.
Creation isn't new—it heals the soul,
Akin to stepping towards a lifelong goal.[2]

---

1. I took a Beatles class during my undergrad, which is where I encountered the story
of Paul McCartney coming up with the tune for "Yesterday" and being concerned that
he stole it from somewhere because it sounded so familiar in his head.
2. I find the gap between the music I perform and the music I write to be
intimidatingly and embarrassingly wide, but one must start somewhere.

Take the Heat

September 14th

September has a sickness and has laid
Upon the air, which moves but won't abate
The listlessness and weakness that pervade
As heat and heaviness on all conflate.
The evening cool and morning dew imply
That fever may have broken in the night,
But as the sun ascends the morning sky,
Pernicious illness manifests its might.
No balm may blunt its incandescent force,
No cure delirium alleviates,
One can but let the ailment run its course
While one's own symptoms one self-medicates:
With water and umbrella repositioning,
As well as finding public air conditioning.[1]

---

1. Days hot enough to make me wish I had air conditioning are rare in San Diego, but there are usually one or two in late summer.

Skimmers[1]

September 15th

To purchase shorts in summer is a task
Best suited to the patient and the mad,
For store employees shrug whenever asked,
And point you at the clearance racks. Too bad
Your choices there are generally restricted
To Daisy Dukes[2] with rhinestone snaps in sizes
Too small and large and with odd flaws afflicted—
Predicting fit's a futile exercise.
Attempting your size guesstimates in styles
That actually expose a bit of knee,
And finding one—hooray!—that isn't vile,
Means plunking plastic down in victory.
I hope the pearls I wear with them begin
To downplay my resemblance to Huck Finn.[3]

---

1. Ladies' cropped trousers.
2. Short, tight denim shorts, often cutoffs, popularized by Daisy Mae Duke in the television show *The Dukes of Hazzard.* Suffice it to say, they are not office-appropriate.
3. Fictional Mark Twain character, a homeless adolescent who lives off the donations of others.

A Brave Front[1]

September 16th

I spoke a dare aloud while raindrops fell
In golden straws and gentle sidewalk spots,
And as the shower waned, I might have yelled
Unto the thunder "Is that all you've got?"
But then a blast of wind flung dust and leaves
And banged recycling bin lids in defiance.
As residents crouched underneath their eaves,
On courtesy we could have no reliance.
And when the heavens opened, washing all
The grit and listlessness from noontime swelter,
Refreshed and by the glorious storm enthralled,
I laughed and didn't rue the lack of shelter.
A salmon sunset met us at the door
My clothes left shining puddles on the floor.[2]

---

1. Wordplay on "brave front," meaning to face something unflinchingly, and a powerful weather front.
2. Though I was exhilarated by walking through the storm, the dogs were decidedly less enthusiastic about the experience.

Solve for X[1]

September 17th

Ten years ago today we two were wed,
And seventeen last June was our first date.
And fifteen years in August our homestead
We made on my arrival in your state.
Next year will be the equinox of years
Spent with you and without you in my life,
The next year's yours, and if we persevere,
Our future will with multiples be rife.
But when I cast my net of reverie
Into the past, no numbers can describe
The depth of love, nor its immensity——
In formulae it cannot be inscribed.
For digits can't describe how love can last,
Or how it makes us feel no time has passed.

---

1. Wordplay involving X, the standard variable in simple linear equations, which is also the Roman numeral ten, which I felt was appropriate for my tenth wedding anniversary.

Boast with the Most, or, In the Mead Hall[1]

September 18th

The hallowed land of Lincoln was my home,
My father's house of mighty logs was built
With watchful eye the acres I did roam
Preventing blameless blood from being spilt.
Each day as I would tread the twisting trails,
I sent a dozen songs out on the breeze—
My merry music made the wicked quail
And charmed the very squirrels from their trees.
From forest to great lake ambition spurred,
And finally, a kingdom by the sea.
My wit, my melodies, and winsome words,
Shall everlasting glory guarantee.
Here in the land of saints and gilded men
I raise my voice and bravely wield my pen.

---

1. Written for a friend whose English class were reading *Beowulf* and were assigned to write heroic, formal boasts of at least ten verse lines, containing two kennings and three examples of alliteration.

Dead Men Tell No Whatsits[1]

September 19th

West County be me dialect, me gait
Is not unlike the rolling of the swells,
And this wide world I'd circumnavigate
To take a richly laden caravel.
I give no quarter, nor expect I none
From vessels I attack, and I'll be blowed
To see me salty crewmates thus undone
By craven coves who keep not to the code.
So if me Jolly Roger should ye see
Surrender, and for my great mercy thank
Your gods that none of ye had chance to flee,
Or else ye and your crew would walk the plank.
And if me cadences I overplay,
I blame it on Talk Like a Pirate Day.

---

1. Talk Like a Pirate Day is a wonderfully silly annual observance invented by
humorist Dave Barry. The title is bastardized from the proverb "Dead men tell no
tales," which features prominently in the Pirates of the Caribbean ride at Disneyland.

Steps in the Right Direction

September 20th

I so look forward to each Saturday
Not just since sleepings-in the days enhance,
But also since I plan two hours to play
And sweat with those who also love to dance.
We work the choreography, then drill
The basics, stretch, and run the dances slated
For future fairs and restaurant gigs, instill
The staging so we'll be coordinated.[1]
But oh, the joy of frolicking in time
Within a motley group who find expression
In rhythm, strength, and gracefulness sublime,
And equally anticipate each lesson.
Our pleasure in the work is so abundant
That audiences almost feel redundant.

---

1. Every performance space is different, so we have to rehearse staging to
accommodate it and the number of dancers available to perform. Changes in staging
can mean that you're performing new choreography.

Day of Rest

September 21st

Can one be said to truly be alone
When one is being lain upon by dogs
Until they bark at passers-by unknown
And neighbors out for their respective jogs?
No. Solitude's the proper name for this,
Now liberated from all obligation,
Except for those I've chosen. I don't miss
The trappings of external expectation,
But bliss and boredom cannot coexist,
And guilt that I relax while others work[1]
Cannot be expeditiously dismissed
Without the niggling fear that I'm a jerk.
I justify indulging selfish wishes
By rolling up my sleeves and doing dishes.

---

1. Justifying taking needed time for self-care can be difficult, particularly for someone who likes being busy.

In Which I Am Self-Deprecating and Meta

September 22nd

When so much happens in a single day
That fourteen lines cannot contain it all,
I must cut ruthlessly joy and dismay
That seem on recollection more banal
Than simple pleasures,[1] grumpy anecdotes,[2]
From which my pithy aphorisms spring;
Fun to extemporaneously quote,
Thus needful, therefore to those words I cling.
But my desire to tell things as they are,
Then wars with my desire to elevate
The daily grind, and so I raise the bar,
And then regret ambition far too late,
And such pretension truly is a yawn—it's
Not like we really need sonnets on sonnets.

---

1. Singing with friends, having a good day at work.
2. Some work frustrations are, of course, inevitable.

Testing

September 23rd

As one who rides the bus to work each day,
I'm quite familiar with that type of rider
Whose seat-bound bag is often in my way,
And sprawling knees expand his quarter wider.[1]
I'm hardly shy—I meet his eyes and smile.
He acts surprised to find I wish to sit,
Oblivious to crowding in the aisle
Until I prompted him to notice it.
To walk like royalty, said Charlize Theron,[2]
You gird your loins and rotate back the shoulders,
Extend your neck as graceful as a heron,
Imagine MURDER—and you'll seem far bolder.
I did and fixed my eye on one young man.
He squeaked "Excuse me!" just before he ran.

---

1. Though this has become popularly known as "manspreading," the behavior isn't strictly exclusive to men.
2. A friend sent me a video of Charlize Theron talking about how she played the evil queen in *Snow White and the Huntsman.* "You have to come from your core, really tight, shoulders down, neck long, and then just think 'Murder,' and walk."

She for #HeForShe[1]

September 24th

A he for she means he's a he for me,
With masculinity, a he can be
In favor of a she's equality
And I'm for him who is a he for she,
A he for she seems elementary
Since codifying femininity,
Will limit every he as well as she.
In patriarchy, violent cruelty
Can visit any she for being she,
But weakness is its own rigidity,
For when he stands with she unsilently,
It shatters tacit solidarity.
Henceforth a she for hes for she I'll be,
In gratitude for spoken empathy.

---

1. A response to Goodwill Ambassador Emma Watson's speech introducing
#HeForShe, a solidarity movement for gender equality, at the United Nations.
Another sonnet featuring a single end rhyme throughout.

Acquainted with the Sunrise[1]

September 25th

Encountering a snapshot of the past,
Can generate nostalgic introspection,
As one finds things that render one aghast
But also joy in those small imperfections,
Because it means that it was truly real.
As you grow chronologically apart
From writing, objectivity anneals
Reproachful mind and then forgiving heart.
It's sad that it's so easy to believe
Your finest efforts are now far behind,
Despite the little wobbles you perceive,
You feel that from your greatness you're confined.
Despite unpleasant musings, persevere—
Six months from now, how wise this will appear![2]

---

1. A riff on Robert Frost's poem "Acquainted with the Night," which also refers to
Ola Gjeilo's *Sunrise Mass,* a recording of which inspired this sonnet.
2. Optimism!

A Roll of the Dice[1]

September 26th

Four cups, five dice a-rattle, then upend
The cup and sneak a glance at what's beneath,
And hope those private faces don't portend
A public tell whilst lying through your teeth.
For bidding on the pips you don't possess
Is risky, but an awful lot of fun,
For when the bid is called, whether success
Or failure is achieved relies on one
To play the odds, for one's long-standing friends
Make every gamble seem beyond the pale,
So utilizing some unusual ends
Means hoping that with fortune you'll prevail.
The dwindling cubes too often will conspire
With those who truly wish to call you liar.

---

1. On playing Liar's Dice.

Headcanon[1]

September 27th

When reading Chekhov with an actor's eye
And finding written: "Traraboomdeyay,"
I wondered what Chebutykin[2] meant thereby,
And what, if anything, he wished to say.
And just what Ronald Hingley[3] heard him sing
When he transcribed the singing from the Russian.
Was he deliberately altering
The onomatopoeia for discussion
To draw a parallel between the man
Who loved the sisters' mother and a duke
Who only loved the chase and crooked plans
That Verdi sought to tacitly rebuke?
So when the doctor sings within the play,
I always hear "La Donna è Mobile."[4]

---

1. Fandom term used by followers of entertainment media (the canon) to describe
something that they believe to be true, even though it has not actually been explicitly
verified by the media.
2. Character from Anton Chekhov's play *Three Sisters*.
3. Russian literature scholar and historian who translated the Chekhov edition I was
reading.
4. Famous aria from Giuseppe Verdi's opera *Rigoletto*, which is sung by the caddish
duke.

Outreach

September 28th

I sang a concert with a hundred friends,
A new conductor, and a brand-new season,
With music that collectively transcends
Chronology, geography, and reason.[1]
Two times my eyes welled up, and twice they spilled;
From Purcell's sorrow[2] and from Bernstein's joy[3]
Philosophy and love were thus fulfilled,
In such a way that time cannot destroy.
Though everyone who heard it will recall,
Its greatest enemy's indifference
Of those who do not have the wherewithal
To actively combat their ignorance.
I only hope that hearing helps them see
We all can own a timeless melody.

---

1. In honor of San Diego Opera's continued existence, San Diego Master Chorale
performed a concert comprised of great opera arias and choruses.
2. Henry Purcell's "When I am Laid in Earth" from *Dido and Aeneas.*
3. Leonard Bernstein's "Make Our Garden Grow" from *Candide.*

Cosmetic Changes

September 29th

Some mornings, through lush breeze and sunlit air,
Demand one view them through unpainted eyes,
Since wind feels freshest kissing skin that's bare,
Suppressed by artifice and wan disguise.
What does the morning care if you've a spot
Or if the skin beneath your eyes is dark?
When such a day's beginning to be wrought,
One must be open to receive its spark.
But when I try to greet the world barefaced
It looks away from my unvarnished flaws,
As if it seeks my substance to erase,
Implying that from sight I should withdraw.
But then a flicker from a treasured friend
Rekindles that with which the dark contends.[1]

---

1. Those capable of brightening a Monday morning are worth their weight in gold.

Mental Health Day[1]

September 30th

Dear Place of Work, Ms. Weber won't be in
Today, tomorrow, possibly all week.
She suffers from a lack of keratin
Upon her toes, and maladies unique:
I diagnose presymptomatic states
Pertaining to her oddly sound psychosis:
Ideopathic syndrome, which dictates
A somewhat unpredictable prognosis.
And therefore, I prescribe a regimen
Of neuroactive exercises, such
As media that features certain men
Exemplifying attributes nonesuch.
I recommend the treatment start forthwith.
Respectfully, Sincerely, Dr. Smith.

---

1. A good thing to do after an exhausting performance weekend is to take a sick day. I couldn't on that day, unfortunately, but at least I had fun thinking about it.

October

A Delicate Balance

October 1st

Once past the equinox, the sun's bright rays
Diminish, angles narrowing, acute,
So one must change the starts and ends of days,
Adjusting to dark dressing and commute,
As well as changing schedules and new students,
And brand new quarter, weather, term, and season.
So greet the changes with sufficient prudence
To understand the difference and the reason:
For when one's judgment wars with intuition,
With all too many variables in play,
The wisest path's avoiding admonition,
And all reactions carefully assay.
One cannot elevate one's pride and vanity
At the expense of peace of mind and sanity.[1]

---

1. This refers to one of my periodic freak-outs that occurs during periods of
adjustment to new schedules, during which I manage to convince myself that I've said
"yes" to too many optional activities (I probably had). This particular bout of self-
recrimination occurred because I'd had a memory lapse in which I offered to give a
friend a ride home from work and forgotten that I'd chosen to take the bus that
morning. Thankfully, she has an excellent sense of humor and a bus pass.

Spineless

October 2nd

Just yesterday I opened up a book[1]
Beloved by those whose taste I know and trust,
And fifteen minutes later I was hooked—
Engrossed as to the daily grind I bussed.
Fatigue and miscommunications kept
Me from advancing further in the story
But that night as I closed my eyes and slept,
I hunted, and the novel was my quarry.
This morning on the bus, my bag revealed
No longed-for tale. I found myself unable
My self-exasperation to conceal
Recalling that the book was on the table.
Such busy days and too-exhausted nights
Can lead to disappointing oversights.

---

1. Bryce Courtenay's engrossing book *The Power of One.*

The Other Shoe[1]

October 3rd

I must protest: it's not procrastination—
It's effort that's expended to prevent
Redundancy; to hamper duplication
Of tasks, uncertainty to circumvent.
For what's the point of jumping when I'm told
When quick responses lead to admiration
For just as long as praise takes to grow cold
And lead to a delayed realization?
Oh no! This won't work after all! Redo
These tasks and find a preferable solution
Accommodating what I sort-of-knew.
You have eight hours to find a resolution.
Who knows if I'd experience less pique
If these things didn't happen every week?[2]

---

1. The history of the phrase "waiting for the other shoe to drop," meaning to be in
anticipation of something that past experience has taught you will probably occur,
may be found in footnote 2 of "True, Not Free" (July 16th).
2. There is such a thing as scheduling something too far in advance.

The A Train

October 4th

When working on a problem of some size
There sometimes comes a flash of clarity
That makes all your preceding steps seem wise,
And your conclusions ring with verity—
For suddenly, the path is not defined
By dead ends that in error you have taken,
Instead, mistakes seem perfectly designed
A vital new perspective to awaken.[1]
It is impossible to trust perfection,
For fear of failure's thoroughly enmeshed
So even when one speaks with circumspection
The fear of overstatement breeds afresh.
Try not to think about the destination—
Instead, try to enjoy the exploration.

---

1. When I'm writing, I refer to this moment as Magic Eye, because suddenly it's as if the fog lifts and you can clearly see the path laid out before you, and you see how what you've done thus far can be connected to where you want to be.

Away[1]

October 5th

A half-read book beneath a ceiling fan,
A stoneware mug that's full of IPA
But sleepy hounds do not complete the clan,
The house feels empty when you are away.
The hummingbirds squeak disapprovingly
At roaring F/A-18s[2] on display
And football contests only bring ennui—
The house feels silent when you are away.
My aches and weariness may dissipate
From resting through an online holiday,
In solitude, stress can evaporate.
Could it do so if you were not away?[3]
Through mindfulness and self-care will I earn
The heartfelt joy I feel at your return.

---

1. My spouse worked on an unexpected Sunday, and I missed him.
2. The McDonnell Douglas F/A-18 Hornet is a supersonic combat jet used by the US military.
3. And yet sometimes solitude is exactly what I need to face the coming weeks (and months).

The Gracious Month[1]

October 6th

Such mild commencement to a hectic day
Is proof variable nature can be kind,
With offerings of dew that cool my feet
And unexpected blooms in autumn's heat.
Deciduous decay and blossoms sweet
In temperate October are combined.
The daytime warmth begs summertime to stay
As falling darkness pushes it away.
Not even California can delay
Earth's unrelenting angle nor defeat
The system our sun's gravity aligned,
So to the shifting seasons we're resigned.
I feel the sunlight growing less intense,
And jack-o-lanterns' ample recompense.

---

1. An October appreciation sonnet. Since the theme was seasonal rotation, I rotated
end rhymes and couplets in the stanzas.

Dyschronous

October 7th

The eastern clouds masked daybreak's glow so well
All sources of the blue-grey light were blurring.
Without a timepiece, it was hard to tell
If sunrise or a sunset was occurring.
And in the evening, six musicians wrought
Hypnotic aural waves from wooden planks.[1]
Painstaking polyrhythmic patterns sought
To cloud the consciousness, and left a blank.
So often on a chosen holiday[2]
The contexts with which every day is greeted
That frame my thoughts and actions go away,
Ambitious plans too often uncompleted.
But since, from sunrise, I checked expectations,
There were no limits to my aspirations.

---

1. The Los Angeles Philharmonic's Green Umbrella concert "Percussion Marvels,"
which included David Lang's *the so-called laws of nature* and Michael Gordon's
Timber, which is played by six percussionists on two-by-fours.
2. Since work was exhausting and I had many performances on the horizon, I decided
to take a preventative sick day.

Klavierstruck[1]

October 8th

Was it rehearsing music in the day
That set afire the music in my mind?
Or was it last night's concert in L.A.
That left enduring vestiges behind?
While Handel haunts my projects yet undone
And Johnny Cash accompanies my rise
In elevators, what would be the fun
Of contradicting all that it implies:
Two types of music, one that soothes and sends
The mind to calmer states, and one whose strains
Inspires new enterprises and depends
On time and space the vision to sustain.
I dare not limit inspiration's scope—
All I can do is write it down and hope.

---

1. Pun on Karlheinz Stockhausen's *Klavierstücke (Piano Pieces)*.

Subjunctive

October 9th

Scientia potentia est wrote Hobbes;
In knowledge there is power, this is true;
Judicious exercise can make our jobs
Efficient, fun, and possible to do.
It thrusts a certain order on the mind
Connecting discrete problems and solutions,
So when bad luck and chaos are combined
They bring about my wisdom's evolution.
Thus, problems that I don't anticipate,
Are often solvable with proven tricks,
And while they might not totally negate
The issues, they're a tolerable fix.
I know the thought is futile, but how grand
That day would be when all would go as planned![1]

---

1. Work was about twice as busy as usual, and I was feeling the strain.

Such a Lovely Audience[1]

October 10th

I dropped a quote into the internet,[2]
As witness to a fairly brutal week.
Though posting my frustrations did offset,
No serious discussion did I seek.
I pirouetted in a passageway
For love of slickness of a leather sole
On waxed linoleum and of the day—
To be observed was not at all the goal.
Both times I met an unexpected smile
From someone who provided recognition
Of Friday joy and wordplay versatile,
Quixotically, quite of his own volition.
Though threats to privacy may cause unease,
Sometimes it can be nice when someone sees.

---

1. From the Beatles' song "Sgt. Pepper's Lonely Hearts Club Band."
2. I quoted *The Princess Bride*. Copious counter-quotes from friends were heartening.

Elephantine[1]

October 11th

A pachyderm, as naming would imply,
Is quite encompassed by a rugged hide.
Alas, that epithet must needs belie
The tenderness the creature keeps inside.
Enormity and strength too often tempt
Some smaller, weaker entity to force
Them into yoke; their seizure will exempt
The captor from all pity and remorse.
And even those who freely range are caught
In land disputes and shrinking territory,
Or for their ivory are coldly shot
By those for whom blood money is the quarry.
Until peace gives them refuge overdue
I'm glad they find kind treatment at the zoo.[2]

---

1. Another Early Zoo day at the San Diego Zoo that I was awake enough to attend.
See "The Finch Response" (June 14th).
2. Due to the collective experience of the elephant keepers and San Diego's mild
climate, the San Diego Zoo has become a refuge for geriatric elephants.

Versa Vice[1]

October 12th

This evening, driving over to the pub,
We saw that we had already arrived,
For parked fortuitously near a shrub,
The model, make, and color that we drive.
And since the street had no more empty space,
With our past selves we felt a little vexed
That by their lingering we were displaced,
Who knew what inconvenience they'd cause next?
But then, upon a cross street I espied
A space much closer to our destination.
We slid into it with a dash of pride
That really didn't bear examination.
We had to laugh at our desire to thwart
Our own extrapolated selves for sport.

---

1. Pun on the model of our car (Nissan Versa), a vehicle popular enough that we probably shouldn't derive as much glee from yelling "Twin car!" when we see one like ours.

Mutinous[1]

October 13th

I cannot blame the captain of the ship
For disciplining lubberly midshipmen,
Though crews through which misunderstanding slip
With noxious rumors thoroughly equip men.
Suspicion sowed on every spar and deck
Makes all desirous of assigning blame
In order to avert a violent wreck,
Unlucky Jonah[2] being called by name.
So when the purser gets a private note,
Requesting guidance, he does not return it.
Instead he will betray the one who wrote
And make him wish that he had thought to burn it.
From whom will superstition ask a price—
The purser or the one who sought advice?

---

1. Extended nautical metaphor for an annoying kerfuffle at my job.
2. Nickname for an unlucky crew member, from the Biblical story of Jonah, who flees
from God only to end up swallowed by a giant fish (or whale).

Tech Week, Part 1[1]

October 14th

To be a part of premiering a show[2]
Though as I am, quite peripherally,[3]
Is like a foxtrot: slow, slow, quick-quick, slow—
A slog until it runs, not magically,
Because you saw each portion of the trick
Rehearsed, repeated, every cue perfected,
Until at last each tiny cog will click
Into its proper place, interconnected,
Or proximal—oh let it not be long,
Before the show is ready to be run
So there is time for all things to go wrong
Before it will be seen by everyone![4]
And once performance fears are realized
They'll seem less terrifying in your eyes.

---

1. Tech week (or often weeks) is the painstaking process of adding lights, sound, special effects, and other final polishes to a production in the run-up to previews and opening night.
2. Disney Theatrical and La Jolla Playhouse's US premiere of Alan Menken and Stephen Schwartz's *Hunchback of Notre Dame.*
3. Each performance required 32 choristers, who were placed at the back of the set in monastic robes and fill out the musical score. We had more singers than spaces per performance, so we had "teams" that rotated rehearsals and performances, which means that I only had to sit through a couple of painstaking tech rehearsals.
4. It never quite happens that way, but it's a nice thought.

An Incoherent Whatsit[1]

October 15th

Too long my work day stretched into the dusk—
And thanks to that, plucked shelving coasted free,
And bustled flimsy sausages with musk
Whilst funding porridge uniformity.
The tasks undone left my exhausted brain
In gabled tortoises of clearest loam,
Foretold acrostic corduroy terrain,
And shortly cracked the unsung magic chrome.
If needing sense or judgment, come not here—
The bungees of my brain are clearly flocked.
It's all that I could do to engineer
A belly button when the phantom squawked.
As zebras drive all rhubarb on the cheap,
One hopes antiques dance cromulent[2] with sleep.

---

1. I found it surprisingly difficult to write lines that have proper grammar and word usage while still making zero sense. That may, of course, have been partially due to exhaustion.
2. A word coined on *The Simpsons* to mean "legitimate," but it's used in a knowingly ironic way to indicate that the "legitimate" claim is, in reality, malarkey.

Rather Nice[1]

October 16th

The best laid plans, as Rabbie[2] said, go wrong
And leave us feeling saddened and distressed—
One has but little choice to go along
And hope the plans survive the latest test.
Though one can't guess the vagaries of fate,
One can design a strategy robust
In which contingencies are given weight,
Statistics leaving fortune quite nonplussed.
But when a plan is lacking from inception
And your resources cannot be sufficient
To fix it, your selective self-deception
Convinces you you're actually omniscient.
But no: on fickle luck you are dependent
And if not luck, his taciturn attendant.

---

1. From Rose Amy Fyleman's poem "Mice."
2. Refers to Robert Burns's "To a Mouse," whose famous line "The best laid schemes
o' Mice an' Men/Gang aft agley..." is paraphrased here.

Exhausting Week

October 17th

I knew this week was going to be unpleasant—
The only thing unknown was the degree
To which the lousiness was clear and present
And how long I'd endure ignominy.
Between bad news and stress I had my pick,
With fraught misunderstandings in between,
And each that followed felt like one more kick
From fortune's well-oiled ass-kicking machine.
Some unexpected kindnesses were granted,
Because, most likely, chance already found
Incessant misery should be supplanted:
Because you can't trip someone on the ground.
Long weeks and days will sleepy Libbys make
I've no idea how I'm still *zzzzzzzzzzzzzzzzzzzzzzzzzz*[1]

---

1. A rare deliberate break in scansion (several inadvertent ones persist), though a
rhyming/scanning word may be easily inferred.

Bough Wow Rough Roof[1]

October 18th

I like to think that dogs are quite amazed
At how their owners can communicate
If actions should be scolded or be praised,
And if it means their supper should be late.
For while they exercise precise olfaction,
Anatomy their vocal skill impedes.
Domestication modified attraction
To humans and the skill to guess their needs.
Are whines a dog's attempted conversation,
Or simply treats and dinner to beseech?
Or possibly a puerile imitation
Of what's perceived when they hear human speech?
Regardless of how they see what we say,
We understand each other anyway.

---

1. Fun with homophones intended to highlight the similarity between the sounds dogs make and human speech.

Widow Dido[1]

October 19th

Dido's Lament,[2] that melody immortal,
Premiered within a girls' school's cloistered walls,
And functions as a chronomobile portal—
Contemporary listeners[3] might forestall
The tragedy by asking what went wrong,
Exactly how the queen of Carthage died—
Did Dido droop to death[4] as in the song,
Or was it star-crossed lover's suicide?
I like to think the pyre on which she burned
To tell Aeneas "Hi!" was just a ruse
That through enforced experience was earned,
So later she could do what she would choose.
And in my mind her romances thereafter
Did fill her life with wisdom, joy, and laughter.[5]

---

1. From Shakespeare's *The Tempest,* act 2, scene 1.
2. The aria "When I am laid in earth" from Henry Purcell's opera *Dido and Aeneas.*
3. This sonnet was inspired by a San Diego Master Chorale concert, under the direction of Dr. John Russell, in which we performed selections from *Dido and Aeneas.*
4. Observation courtesy Dr. Gary McKercher, who commented that the chorus after "When I am laid in earth," which is "With drooping wings ye Cupids come," might offer hints as to Dido's cause of death.
5. See "Headcanon" from September 27th.

We're All Mad Here[1]

October 20th

It's odd to me that there's a time of year
When we're at peace with skeletons on doors,
Where ghouls elicit smiles instead of fear,
And everybody suddenly adores
The spider webs that they'd fain brush away
In any other month, and recreate
In pristine homes a semblance of decay,
Suburban normalcy to desecrate.
And while a cynic might turn up his nose,
I can't not be delighted by the sight
Of all the weird with boring juxtaposed
For weeks on end—not just a single night.
I know, behind each spicy pumpkin drink,
We all have more in common than we think.

---

1. From Lewis Carroll's *Alice's Adventures in Wonderland*, and intended to call attention to the way that Halloween traditions would be considered odd if divorced from their context.

Still I Rose[1]

October 21st

From barren soil a tender tendril sprouted—
To coax it into blooming I did yearn.
What sort it was; I never thought about it—
The plant's survival was my chief concern.
When one leaf-swaddled bud began to swell,
My joy unfurled, and in those ardent throes,
I hoped my wishes blossoms would compel,
And—finally!—appeared a large pink rose.
Pink roses? Those clichés of trite romance?
That's what my careful tending has produced?
No fragrant lily gave my plot a glance,
Nor fragile orchid my designs seduce?
Yet roses grew where carefully I tended
Who is to say that isn't what's impended?[2]

---

1. Punning on Maya Angelou's "Still I Rise."
2. Inspired by my dismay at having deliberately written an artistic cliché, despite knowing that thematically, lyrically, and plot-wise it needed to be there.

308

Corvid[1] Composition

October 22nd

Four ravens sat upon a branch's vee
Attempting to usurp the prime position,
All croaking in four-part polyphony
As if rehearsing for a crow audition
In which their size conferred no special edge,
Requiring the quartet to hone the skill
That might just help their common dream to fledge—
But feuds for fame are always fought uphill.
As I admired their robes of shining black
That whispered as if made from finest silk,
My close attention took them all aback,
Appropriately distrustful of my ilk.[2]
If they retain their native-born suspicion,
Their music will outlive their competition.

---

1. Corvidae is the family that contains crows, ravens, rooks, and other nifty species of bird.
2. Though I'm sad when birds fly away because I've stopped to watch them, the moment when they realize I'm there is often very funny.

The Fangirl's Progress[1]

October 24th

My seven-year-old self would be amazed
To know adult-me met C-3PO,[2]
And at his feet appeared both pleased but dazed
Whilst singing backup for him in a show.
Obsessive teen-me, Disney superfan,
Would envy grown-up-me as she disports
While Alan Menken gives notes on a plan
To add new choral songs to Stephen Schwartz.[3]
To see my youthful yearnings grow and bloom,
Some decades later, makes me rather thrilled—
It makes me certain I should not presume
To guess which current dreams may be fulfilled.
Tonight, I need no hindsight to attest
That Libbys past and present are impressed.

---

1. A play on Igor Stravinsky's opera *The Rake's Progress*, which was inspired by
William Hogarth's paintings and engravings of the same name.
2. Anthony Daniels, the actor who played the droid C-3PO in the *Star Wars* movies,
gave the San Diego Master Chorale singers a delightful pep talk prior to our *Star
Wars in Concert* performance in May of 2010.
3. During the sitzprobe for *Hunchback of Notre Dame*, Alan Menken and Stephen
Schwartz discussed adding the chorus to one of Frollo's songs, since in that moment,
Frollo believes that the orders he's giving are divine in origin.

Table Read[1]

October 24th

Today, I tried to see if I was able
To write a sonnet in a new location,
Specifically, our humble kitchen table,
Where we indulge in games and fine gustation.
One might not think that space has an effect
On whether one can do cerebral work,
But here desire and habit intersect,
And it's enough to make one go berserk—
For in my deep blue bedroom or the bus
The visual and aural cues bring calm.
But here, distractions will demand of us
Attention, and ignoring them's no balm.
Success is but a Pyrrhic victory
That proves me skilled in mediocrity.[2]

---

1. A table read is an early stage of a television/film/theatre production in which the
cast reads through the screenplay/script for the first time, usually seated at a table.
2. This sonnet underscored my frustration that I didn't have a dedicated writing space,
as described in Virginia Woolf's essay *A Room of One's Own*, despite having
expressed a desire for one for many years.

Putting It Together[1]

October 25th

The sitzprobe[2] for the first time let us hear
The contribution choral singers make
And how in scenes of drama we appear
To underscore precisely what's at stake.
Tonight's invited dress, our first time through
Without a pause and for a friendly crowd,
Which plunged us into darkness without view,
But we with great perspective were endowed—
For though there was new music to be sung
That we'd scant opportunity to learn[3]
It slid into its place when bells were rung—
We did our part to help make Paris burn.
Our faith has been repaid, for now we know
That we've helped make a really awesome show.[4]

---

1. Title comes from Stephen Sondheim's *Sunday in the Park with George.*
2. Literally "seated rehearsal," the part of a musical or opera production when the orchestra, chorus/ensemble, and principal cast run through all of the music in the show.
3. Despite the hopes expressed in "Tech Week, Part 1" (October 14th), we were still receiving revisions throughout the preview performances.
4. It was a thrill to see the whole show come together, even from my place in the rafters.

Simple Gifts

October 26th

Just ask: it shall be granted unto you,
Is something I was told when I was small.
Internalized through song, I therefore knew
That wanting was sufficient wherewithal.
I quickly learned that it was perilous
To yearn when perspicacity is lacking,
As those who listened could be querulous
And wear when one anticipated tacking.[1]
Philosophers would argue without blinking
Such bargaining's a formal fallacy
Or worse, a magical excuse for thinking,
And yet my simple heart cannot agree.
When need turns into money in the bank,
It's lovely to have multitudes to thank.[2]

---

1. Nautical terms for turning a sailing vessel.
2. Though I was unable to negotiate a pay raise in order to offset new and unexpected transportation costs at work, I was offered a singing job that covered several months of the increased cost, for which I was enormously grateful.

"Poor Me" Syndrome[1]

October 27th

When naps are insufficient to restore
One's equipoise and sordid things enthrall,
Contentious arguments make pride grow sore——
The calendar illuminates it all.
When copious caffeine gives one the shakes,
From snide remarks it's harder to abstain,
And twaddle seems to have the highest stakes——
The calendar endeavors to explain:
The days' routines obscure the passing time
And pharmaceuticals can regulate
Sans deference to nature, and so I'm
Oblivious until I see the date.
And once I've clarified my skewed perception,
I celebrate another misconception.

---

1. One of many manifestations of PMS.

Observation

October 28th

As families dependent on a member
Whose work, at any time, may call them in,
Regardless of the time and day remember
It's not the date; it's what's observed therein.[1]
An anniversary may see delay
Until it can be nicely celebrated
And any gift, regardless of the day,
Will be enjoyed and much anticipated.
Observances are simply that: observed
At times in which they're deemed to be convenient.
Provided that the spirit is preserved,
Do not condemn the letter, and be lenient.
I celebrate three hundred sonnets done,
Observing it in sonnet three-oh-one.

---

1. My husband and I are both children of physicians, whose call schedule sometimes
dictated delayed holiday celebrations.

A Change in the Weather[1]

October 29th

When one is pounded by a hurricane
Awaiting the arrival of the eye
While buffeted by wind and soaked by rain,
Enduring for the promised calm nearby,
It's quite dismaying when that longed-for peace
Neglects to come and callously implodes,
An unexpected hurricane's surcease
Chaotic, savage thunderstorm forebodes.
But weather cannot be controlled by yearning,
So batten hatches down as best you can.
It's really more annoying than concerning
To make impromptu changes to your plan.
So keep a weather eye and don't despair—
Somebody's likely laughing hard somewhere.

---

1. A line from "The Surrey with the Fringe on Top" from Rogers and Hammerstein's *Oklahoma!*. This sonnet is a metaphor for agitated, tempestuous schedules.

Dreams and Schemes[1]

October 30th

The sheeting nimbus, redolent of rain,
And crowns of cumulus turned fiery rose
Beneath the wispy cirrus entertain——
Illuminated structures that compose
A sunset of confusion, all ablaze,
With altocumulus in fluffy grids
And cirrostratus fading into haze——
Such chaos Occam's Razor would forbid.
And yet the sky and I are of one mind:
Too many wonders live beneath the sun
To be to dull sequential tasks confined,
So bring on everything at once for fun!
So I progress through wonders that abound
Sustained by hope that I won't run aground.

---

1. From Joni Mitchell's song "Clouds."

Cloud Allusions I Recall[1]

October 31st

Bright Star,[2] a musical collaboration
Between Steve Martin and Edie Brickell,
Whose title comes from Keats,[3] whose exhortation
Tells paramours in patience they should dwell,
Competes with Randall Thompson for delight,
Whose setting of "Choose Something Like a Star"
By Robert Frost, with Keats's Eremite,[4]
One seen up close and one seen from afar.
But who's to say two works that might allude
With learned respect to one immortal piece
That by chronology one might preclude
The other's fame, its prominence decrease?
For truly, one shared thought can be a treat
When it will complement and not compete.

---

1. Pun on a lyric from Joni Mitchell's song "Clouds."
2. The Old Globe's premiere of Steve Martin and Edie Brickell's bluegrass musical *Bright Star.*
3. Refers to John Keats's "Bright star, would I were stedfast as thou art".
4. From the above poem by Keats, "Like nature's patient, sleepless Eremite...."

November

Midterm[1]

November 1st

Like Brooks's Crazy Woman[2] will I look
At this eleventh month with certain glee,
Although the song I sing won't be mistook
For dissidence, just yearning to be free
From regular bombardment by the phone,
The radio, TV, mail, door to door—
All seeking to condemn or to condone
Opinions they would normally ignore.
But when my ballot's cast, the calls will cease,
The lobbying machine will disappear,
Or hibernate and gradually increase
To burst forth in the next election year.
'Gainst countless candidates and propositions,
Good sources are the strongest oppositions.

---

1. Midterm elections for state and federal congressional seats, local officials, and state and local ballot propositions.
2. Refers to the title character of Gwendolyn Brooks's poem "The Crazy Woman."

All Saints

November 2nd

For all the Saints, who from their Thursday rest[1]
Until next Sunday, when San Francisco
Shall play them as with Lucifer possessed,[2]
For Saints have hands that pilgrims' hands forgo,[3]
All saints must make two miracles occur
To be considered thus by orthodoxy.
But if a mundane wonder one prefers,
Would that not be a kind of paradoxy?
That happenstance that happens to bring joy,
Those grand coincidences that conspire
To bring indulgences that never cloy—
Can such a thing by happy chance transpire?
Such pleasing things fill hearts with gratitude,
Reminding us of our beatitude.

---

1. William Walsham How's hymn "For all the Saints, who from their labor rest."
2. Refers to the NFL football team the New Orleans Saints, who were scheduled to play the San Francisco 49ers.
3. From Shakespeare's *Romeo and Juliet* act 1, scene 5.

321

Time Management

November 3rd

My calendar and I are on good terms:
It tells me where and when and what to be,
And leaves to me deciding what is firm
And what was added arbitrarily,[1]
And so when double bookings do occur,
Inevitable as housework, death, and taxes,
To sanity and wellness I defer
And other limitations learned through praxis.
At this I am not always so successful,
Since sometimes business slips between the cracks,
And sussing out one's loyalties is stressful,
Which leaves a dearth of moments to relax.
But for the nonce, I'll keep an even tread
As long as I don't look too far ahead.

---

1. You'd think by this point in the year, I'd know better than to add things to my performance schedule. Alas, this was not the case.

All for an "I Voted" Sticker

November 4th

My phone was silent in the falling dusk.
No campaign flyers clogged our daily mail.
No nosy pollsters forced me to be brusque,
As they my doors and worried dogs assail.
The only sign that we have reached the end
Of this incessant, scurrilous campaign:
Long lines of cars the polling sites attend
As hopefuls pray their wait won't be in vain.
Now precincts certify and bubbly flows
To celebrate or offer consolation
To challengers, incumbents, and all those
Whose efforts irritated all the nation,
I'm equally annoyed at wins and losses—
I wish campaigns could be thrown out of office.[1]

---

1. And that was just a midterm election!

Sport

November 5th

I tossed the birdie high into the sky,
Then spiked it with my trusty ping-pong paddle.
Alas, my shrewd opponent did decry
The placement of my flag preceding battle.
But lo, he stood in a reversal zone,
And so my penalty on him would fall
Through song and dance my error to atone,
Except I raised aloft the volleyball
And threw it mightily into a tree
Where it did lodge—a most palpable hit[1]
Which made the score chartreuse to forty-three
Until it dawned: my goal was opposite.
For chaos holds insanity in thrall
When one's engaged in playing Calvinball.[2]

---

1. From *Hamlet,* act 5, scene 2.
2. Calvinball is a game invented by Calvin in Bill Watterson's comic strip *Calvin and Hobbes*. The rules are that you make up the rules as you go along and that you can't use rules twice (except for the rule that rules can't be used twice). It usually involves random sporting equipment and black masks.

Hopeless[1]

November 6th

Elections did not go as I had hoped,
Despite the plethora of hopeful signs
So with grave disappointment I must cope...
Aww. Look at that sweet puppy. HE IS MINE!
Alas, perspective is in short supply—
When one is feeling fresh pain and depression;
The war of spite with wishing to comply,
FOR GOODNESS SAKES, DO YOU SEE THAT EXPRESSION???
How can I gaze upon my silly pups
Unsoftened by their love from time to time?
From nearby congregant I'll take the cups,
But puppy kisses might just prove sublime.
So seize the smooches when and where you may—
Because no other day shall be today.

---

1. Refers dually to being without hope politically and to being hopelessly besotted with my dogs.

O My Sainted Aunt[1]

November 7th

My weary feet conveyed me to a wall
Where previously a flight of stairs had been—
A set of rotten roots had caused to fall
A mighty eucalyptus, clad in green.
When morning dawned, the screen of leaves had gone,
The trunk chopped into manageable blocks,
Though metal bannister had undergone
A transformation from the sudden shock.
So when today a much beloved tree
From whose progenitors I also grew
Succumbed to unrelenting gravity,
We in her shade were also knocked askew.
Though we feel broken now, we are protected
And strengthened having been interconnected.

---

1. *In memoriam* my "sainted" Aunt Anne, the Rev. Audrey Evans Lee. Born on August 6th,1943, she passed away on November 7th, 2014. *Requiem aeternam dona eis, Domine, et lux perpetua luceat eis.*

Day of the Living

November 8th

Two women, separated by three years,
Two thousand, seven hundred sixty miles,
And three time zones, but linked by blood and tears
Pick up their phones with matching wistful smiles
And dial the number of their elder brother
To wish him happy birthday both at once,
Thus making him ring off to greet the other
And share amusement at their timely stunts.
Though it may seem a sheer coincidence
For two to reach out quite concurrently,
It's fitting in the context of events
Affecting the entire family.
A day of sharing thoughts of the departed[1]
Makes space for happenstances more lighthearted.

---

1. My brother's birthday was the day after Aunt Anne's passing, so when my sister and I both called him at the same time, we all had a very welcome laugh.

Inner Space

November 9th

Bereavement is a hole that soon appears
Protected by an unapparent seal.
Thus, hidden and immeasurable, one fears
The indefinable may not be real.
And yet it can be felt sporadically,
At times both unforeseeable and those
That fall within predictability
And half-remembered history—suppose
That curiosity will chip away
The seal, but fear of sadness fills the cracks—
Is grief a thing that thinking can allay
Or is it something everything impacts?
There's no one way to meaningful goodbye,
Nor is there a convenient time to cry.[1]

---

1. Fortunately, I am adept at crying in most situations.

Seasonettes

November 10th

When one lives in a coastal chaparral,
The joke is that we only have two seasons:
One dry, one wet, and by that rationale
Our climate is monotonous, and reasons
To shun it are abounding, for the mild
Of winter weakens us when faced with cold,
Expecting it to suit us, like a child,
As if to human wishes climates mold.
Endemic plants cannot hope to compete
With foreign trees and irrigated lawns,
Which means that autumn isn't obsolete—
But rather, in an instant it is gone.
When fall's bright fifteen minutes have been spent,
Then comes our frosty hour of discontent.[1]

---

1. Play on the opening lines of Shakespeare's *Richard III.*

AAK and EEW[1]

November 11th

We met in summer, fathers' daughters we,[2]
Though during school years we were separated,
And parents' hopes were not a guarantee,
We reunited, friendship unabated.
But then one autumn, new names we selected
To be our first identities online,
And since we two were previously connected
The BBS[3] served only to refine
Our giddiness—for once, we weren't just two,
We found like-minded souls around the world,
So "Sophie" and "November" joined the crew,
And motley, joyous freak flags we unfurled.
Though worldly currents sweep us far apart
We both know how to navigate by heart.

---

1. A birthday sonnet for my best friend Aliya.
2. We met because our fathers were working at the same hospital.
3. Our local Bulletin Board Service, which brought the internet to our homes and allowed us to chat into the wee hours of the morning without disturbing our parents, especially once we figured out how to silence our modems.

Big Miss[1]

November 12th

A dachshund's an unsubtle little creature
Whose manners are perfunctory at best,
Whose stubbornness confounds the patient teacher,
By whom a grand persona is possessed.
But luckily, attempts at stealing food
Are oft preceded by a stalking mien,
And throes of undesired solitude
Through yaps and cunning poses can be seen.
While nipped requests in healing take a while,
And naughtiness produces looks contrite
That last a second, then becomes a smile,
Love needn't be well-polished or polite.
On days of politics and half détentes,
It's really nice to know what someone wants.

---

1. Dedicated to Amelia, who first observed of Hildegard, "Unsubtle dachshund is unsubtle." "Big Miss" is one of Hildy's many nicknames.

Reviewing[1]

November 13th

When one performs a musical's premiere
The wait for feedback seems well nigh eternal.
Will critics rave? Will audiences cheer?
Will chipper chatter spread or rants infernal?
Will people sense the spilled ink, sweat, and tears
That brought the show so suddenly to life,
Comprised of Broadway vets and volunteers
Collectively who balance on a knife?
Of course, reaction's mixed: one thoroughly
Adores the luscious score, one finds it trite,
One hates the sad, one hates the comedy,
But great performance makes a pleasant night.
And hearing those discordant points of view
Makes subsequent performances feel new.

---

1. *Hunchback of Notre Dame* officially opened, and the (mostly positive) reviews
rolled in.

Clique Claque[1]

November 14th

When one knows members of the audience,
The show will inexplicably feel fraught,
And one feels one can tell the difference
Between a friendly crowd and one that's not.
Your ears are tuned to laughter and your eyes
Are drawn to those with hands against their faces
Contorted with despair or with surprise,
As they're put through their sentimental paces.
But when the signs are indisputable:
The audience shows no signs of rebelling,
Delusions that become more suitable,
And kind to stories ready for retelling.
For we whose friends are obviously proud,
We'll grin in what few moments it's allowed.

---

1. Claques are audience members paid to loudly respond to a performance, either approvingly or not. I didn't actually pay my family and friends come to see me in *Hunchback*, but I was happy they came anyway.

God Head

November 15th

It's thanks to John and John[1] I know the word
That's used when martyrs are in art depicted
Whilst holding their own severed heads: absurd,
Yet somehow dignified are the afflicted.
It's thanks to Schwartz and Menken[2] I possess
A favorite cephalophore at all.
My past pet peeves they handily redress,
While cleverness and spectacle enthrall.
Though Aphrodisius[3] unfortunate
Capitulated to the mob his head,
His generosity produced a glut
Of miracles performed once he was dead.
When silliness can come from sacrifice
And well-enshrined in song,[4] it's rather nice.

---

1. John Linnell and John Flansburgh of They Might Be Giants. Their song "You Probably Get That a Lot" mentions cephalophores, or head-carrying depictions of saints.
2. Stephen Schwartz and Alan Menken, the lyricist and composer of *Hunchback of Notre Dame* and many other great scores. The version of *Hunchback* we performed included a song sung by a cephalophore named St. Aphrodisius.
3. Saint Aphrodisius, bishop of Beziers, was martyred by pagans and, according to legend, picked up his own severed head and carried it through the city.
4. The song "Flight into Egypt" from *Hunchback,* during which the actor playing St. Aphrodisius removes and replaces his own head.

Nick of Time

November 16th

The faithless hound hides underneath the bed,
Thus showing greater sense than miss and master,
For Dashiell Hammett[1] hit it on the head—
Nora and Nick are quick, but Asta's faster.
My parents, married thirty years and counting,
Diverted by the antics on the screen,
Are laughing, now, as always when surmounting
Their troubles, filling every day between.
As me and mine join in the merriment
I can't not be aware we share the room
With two great pairs, each for the other meant,
One caught in spring, and one in autumn's bloom—
And if we spark so brightly some time yet—
Then, like them, we'll be counted fortunate.

---

1. Refers to the film version of Dashiell Hammet's *The Thin Man*, starring William
Powell and Myrna Loy.

Sudden Stop[1]

November 17th

At first it's preparation, then the work,
Then shifting gears when circumstance requires.
Alas, it is not possible to shirk
Responsibilities when one desires
More sleep or entertainment, but it's not
Maturity that ranks ought over want—
In calculating what, if I get caught,
Will be the penalty, I'm a savant.
So if I disengage from any task,
I do not do it without reservation,
And if you're curious enough to ask,
I'll list ten ways that it's self-preservation.
If not maturity, wisdom perhaps
Will keep me out of time's pernicious traps.

---

1. That day you realize that you really can't do any more in a day than what you've already done.

We Built This Citrus[1]

November 18th

Five years ago we bought a lemon tree
And put it in a smallish square of dirt
Quite unsuspecting that the BBC
Its usefulness with silly would subvert,
Whose groundwork was laid out on our vacations,
With Smotherses[2] and Freberg[3] ever playing,
Developing my aural inclinations
For humor I had small hope of repaying.
But thanks to fandom, I found Cabin Pressure,[4]
I shared it with my folks to pay them back
For years of laughs, in hopes it would feel fresher
In Olney[5] as in Qikiqtarjuaq.[6]
So when my parents flew home yesterday,
They took a lemon, soon to be in play.[7]

1. Feeble wordplay on Starship's *We Built This City.*
2. Comedians Tom and Dick Smothers, known as the Smothers Brothers.
3. Voice actor and radio comedian Stan Freberg.
4. BBC Radio 4 situation comedy series by John Finnemore.
5. My hometown, where my parents live.
6. A small community located on Broughton Island in Canada, known for wildlife watching, featured in an episode of *Cabin Pressure.*
7. Travelling Lemon is a game featured in *Cabin Pressure*, in which contestants take turns hiding a lemon in plain sight to pass the time on long flights.

Sportive Tricks[1]

November 19th

Dog A, once bred to hunt,[2] now pulls and pushes
To search for cats—she would have been aghast
To know that while she hunted we had passed
A cat on leash beyond her well-sniffed bushes.
Dog B, a ratter, bred for killing pests,[3]
Relentlessly pursues discarded food,
And when discovered, loses garbage chewed,
While wholesome sanctioned breakfast he protests.
And Me—I don't know for what I was bred—
Ostensibly, it's not to sit and write,
Producing nothing tangible each night,
And yet, by looking one can be misled—
Wise ancestors by their examples taught
The pointlessness of mourning what I'm not.[4]

---

1. From Shakespeare's *Richard III*, act 1 scene 1.
2. Hildegard is mostly standard dachshund, a breed developed to hunt badgers above and under the ground.
3. Giovanni is at least part schnauzer, a terrier bred to kill rats and act as guard dogs.
4. Since shape and design were central themes to this sonnet, I played with a nonstandard rhyme scheme.

Are We There Yet?[1]

November 21st

A fearsome and delicious spirit, gin,
Which soothes the tongue and warms the weary head,
When mixed with quinine, makes a medicine
Whose thaumaturgy's well-known and widespread.
At least, that's what I'm choosing to believe,
Unwinding from tonight's demanding show,[2]
But from my writing I get no reprieve—
I cannot quit with just a month to go.
Though that remaining month is so congested
That deities would have to intervene
To make me, midst performing, fully rested
At least until we start twenty-fifteen.
I celebrate both couplet and the bottom
Of my fair drink, both transient as autumn.

---

1. One of the few sonnets in which I complain about the sonnet project.
2. We hit that point in the production in which everybody gets sick, including me. Getting through a show when you're willing yourself not to cough and forcing out high notes is a challenge, but can be done with skillful, subtle, and silent deployment of lozenges.

No Problem[1]

November 21st

No Shakespeare text is wholly problem free,
For even *Hamlet* must be saved at sea
By too-convenient pirates at their pleasure—
A text is not a play by any measure.
A play's comprised of options without number
To smooth the moments that the words encumber,
Defining character, gestures explaining
In ways both truthful and yet entertaining.
And when the concept unifies instead
Of playing up the broken story thread,[2]
We understand how *Pericles* can be
A trial to read and yet a joy to see.
For thoughtful, clever work thus on display
Belies the concept of a problem play.

---

1. Reaction to the Old Globe USD Graduate Acting MFA Program's delightful production of Shakespeare's *Pericles, Prince of Tyre*.
2. A reference to the Old Globe's production of *Winter's Tale*, with which I was unimpressed (see "On Disappointing Productions," March 1st).

Eve of Travel[1]

November 22nd

It's vexing when the body's frailty,
Which cannot bear a paucity of slumber
Without succumbing to a malady,
Brings symptoms whose diversions will encumber.
For who has time to sleep when there is singing
Be it a Haydn mass or classic jazz,
Or musicals that leave the spirits ringing—
Experiencing fully what one has?
Alas, how easily one runs aground
When unexpected obstacles arise,
And habit makes one simple to confound
By things far more complex than realized.
If only my dismayed, exhausted stare
Could make frustrations vanish into air.

---

1. Despite my performance commitments, I was able to fly to New York for my Aunt Anne's funeral.

Red Eye[1]

November 23rd

Ten minutes prior to boarding did they say
That I would really, truly have a seat.
At last, my lengthy trip was underway:
Phase One I could potentially complete.
Phase One concluded in the pouring rain,
When hurried ambulation to the gate
Ensured that I could board the Phase Two plane,
Though once on board we had hour's wait.
And now I sit, three hours in advance
Of home until the blessed hour of four
At which the TSA won't look askance
When I pass by as they had done before.
For sustenance and Phase Three wait beyond
The checkpoint ere the new day will have dawned.

---

1. Written during an overnight layover in Buffalo, NY. I felt very fortunate not to be delayed by the enormous blizzard that hit Buffalo the previous week. Fortunately, the snow melted, and I was able to make all of my connections and arrived an hour and a half before the funeral.

Memoriam[1]

November 24th

A celebrant quartet, three sects comprising,
United by their love for the deceased,
Sent offerings of ancient words arising,
In celebration of her life surceased.
A choir of friends, their voices raised in song,
Gave of their music, hallowed ministry,
While consecration with congregant tears
And laughter celebrated memory.
A heartfelt homily, solemn communion
Of which all hearts were welcome to partake,
Clasped hands, sung harmonies, joyful reunion,
And blessed by sudden sun through clouds opaque.[2]
In lines of your experience I read
A life well lived—O Sainted Aunt, Godspeed!

---

1. My Aunt Anne's funeral was excellent, as far as funerals go. She was a retired Presbyterian minister, and each of the celebrants was someone who knew and loved her.
2. My favorite moment of the funeral.

Bequest[1]

November 25th

Four flights to cross the country, none delayed
Except for one that minimized my wait—
The pros and cons, meticulously weighed
Stayed equal, as if part of an estate
That left behind good fortune during travel.
It seems a luxury, yet in this case,
One snag would make the complex trip unravel;
Thus serendipity I did embrace.
When needy, I was given company.
When sorrowed, I had ample space to cry.
When weary, I found rest and reverie.
Now grateful, I accept, not asking why.
Though windfalls pessimists may yet unnerve,
I know not to desire what I deserve.

---

1. An unexpected 24-hours spent in the company of family was balm for the grieving, and good luck with travel was another excellent bequest from my globe-trotting aunt.

Circling

November 26th

When thinking on inevitable ends,
It's easy to neglect the new beginnings,
As focusing on single loss contends
With gratitude for one's abundant winnings.
While evolution doubt will predispose,
Through instinct and a bias negative
That makes us see the spot and not the nose,
We shall endure—we know what makes us live.
So welcome, Dot and Charlotte![1] Bienvenue
To Enid, Mia, Zoe, and to Thomas![2]
Shalom, Olivia and Sonia![3] To
Serena and to Penny[4] I will promise:
Though sorrow may be part of every day,
There always will be good news on the way.

---

1. My newborn second cousins once removed.
2. Another new second cousin once removed and babies of good friends.
3. Babies of my college roommate and my friend and colleague.
4. More babies of friends. What a productive year it was!

Good Day, Sunshine[1]

November 27th

This week has been a time for gratitude
For things like health and love I've never lacked,
But thankfulness for those does not exclude
Appreciation for things less abstract,
Like ample sleep and sunbeams prime for warming,
And wearing shorts while at Thanksgiving feasts
Prepared by those with whom I am performing,
Whilst quoting lines from soldiers, imps, and priests.
For breaking bread with cherished friends and new
While raising voice and glass with equal cheer
The body's strength and spirit will renew,
Serenity will be our souvenir.
My expectations utterly exceeded;
Today was the Thanksgiving that I needed.[2]

---

1. From the Beatles song "Good Day Sunshine."
2. We weren't able to travel because of my performance schedule, but we ended up celebrating Thanksgiving with my friends from the *Hunchback* chorus.

Kumbel[1]

November 28th

It is a most uncommon kind of writer
Whose poems make my sonnets seem loquacious,
And for their brevity shine all the brighter,
Each filled with wit intensely perspicacious.
For who needs fourteen lines when four express
Eternal wisdom on preparing toast,
Then followed by the key to artlessness,
And giving folksy proverbs a riposte?
The facile leaps from silly to profound
Are in the DNA of Piet Hein's grooks,
Which started in the Danish underground,
Now found online and in obscure-ish books.
Like jewels, finely cut and color varied,
I think they'll have a hard time staying buried.

---

1. Kumbel, Old Norse for "tombstone," was the pseudonym of Piet Hein, a Danish polymath who joined the resistance against the Nazis and published poems whose symbolism and allusions allowed him to criticize the occupation without the censors understanding what he was doing. His "grooks" are short, elegant, witty, and often profound.

Under Cover

November 29th

The movie *All About Eve* skews perception
Of understudies, shown as base connivers—
This melodrama is a misconception,
For understudies truly are survivors;
Eight shows a week they stand alert and willing
To fill their usual role or jump into
The shoes of stars who have received top billing,
And will be met with sighs, not ballyhoos,
Which is the reason I am glad to see
The understudies give their parts their all
Be it in title role, or villainy,
On stage, or with us in the practice hall.[1]
So may it be that lucky stars align
And understudies get the chance to shine.

---

1. All of us in the *Hunchback* chorus were particularly fond of the understudy for the villainous Claude Frollo. He would occasionally join our warm-ups to sing Frollo's signature song "Hellfire" with the chorus. He also started the tradition of telling terrible jokes for good luck prior to every show.

The Eyes Have It[1]

November 30th

The eyes, they say, are windows to the soul,
And like them, can fall into disrepair—
The glass obscures and fails to play its role,
The sashes crack, the blinds and curtains tear,
And though such things are easily repaired,
Until the time that all the mending's done,
One must contend with sight that is impaired,
Susceptible to unforgiving sun.
For though the soul exists sans aperture
Allowing light to enter or to leave,
And is adulterated or as pure
As it would be to celebrate or grieve,
Through soul, eye unforgettable appears,
Through eye, the soul can purge itself of tears.

---

1. A pun on "The ayes have it," which is a traditional response in meeting procedure when a motion has enough "aye" votes to carry it.

December

Words of Wisdom[1]

December 1st

If you think hemiola's[2] syncopation,
Inevitably you will enter late.
An audience can hear if there's cessation
Of phrase within a rest. You should abate
Dynamic at the ends of lines Romantic,
In Classical, stay strong until the tonic.
And even if the tempo ends up frantic,
The singers must stay with the philharmonic.
Traditions going back to Bach and Handel,
Which Haydn pilfered, Ludwig Van purloined—
But such sublime homage is never scandal,
For through it different periods are joined.
And knowledge of what forebears thought was pleasant
Illuminates our singing in the present.

---

1. Advice from Maestro Jahja Ling, then music director and conductor of the San Diego Symphony.
2. In music, a seeming shift between duple and triple meter achieved through the grouping of beats rather than a change in time signature.

352

Overdressed

December 2nd

A pair of red galoshes for my feet,
An A-line skirt to ward off puddle splash,
With tights to help retain my bare knees' heat
And extra shoes for when the boots I stash,
A cotton sweater to wick off the damp,
With matching scarf for my cold-roughened throat,
My dapper raincoat, belted like a champ
Combine to make a potent antidote
To hostile elements, and over all
I spread my monumental bumbershoot,
With which I may withstand the wildest squall
Until the hissing, thunderous skies fall mute,
The cataclysm earth and soul revives,
That is, if the predicted rain arrives.[1]

---

1. Alas, the rain didn't arrive until after I returned home, so I was all dressed up with no inclement weather to resist.

Some Enchanted E-vening[1]

December 3rd

You hear a pop and suddenly, a pope
Is seated on a log inside the loge,
The janitor with mop begins to mope
About the dog who's suddenly a doge.
Below, they watch a stag upon the stage
While one man on his date's nape takes a nap,
And since she's on the rag, she's filled with rage,
Her box-mates are agape and mind a gap.
There's far too great a din for them to dine,
And though they'd like to bare all at the bar,
They would much rather win in terms of wine,
Though they will take great care to drive the car.
And through the window grim from built-up grime,
Appears a passerby, prim in her prime.

---

1. Inspired by Tom Lehrer's "Silent E" song, I wrote a sonnet in which each line
contains a word pair consisting of a word with and without silent E (e.g., din/dine,
grim/grime). Also, a play on the song title "Some Enchanted Evening" from Rodgers
and Hammerstein's *South Pacific*.

Stop

December 4th

It started with displays of thoughtlessness,
Which then were amplified by length of day,
Sleep deprivation, and punctiliousness—
It might be good for you to stay away.
Then traffic kept me on the road so long
That I had insufficient time to eat,
And paltry meals serve only to prolong
An awful mood— you really should retreat,
Because if you do not, I will regret
The awful things that I could say to you.
I know what words are likely to upset,
Malicious, spiteful, cruel, but also true.
My thanks for being brave and choosing flight—
At times it's cowardly to stay and fight.[1]

---

1. On times when discretion is the better part of valor. Or, as was sung in *Monty Python and the Holy Grail,* "When danger reared its ugly head, he bravely turned his tail and fled."

Nothing to See

December 5th

Too much occurred today to fit it in
To fourteen lines, and so I'll summarize:
Work wasn't awesome, much to my chagrin,
But I excelled when left to improvise.
By contrast, in the evening I adhered
To notes and the notation on the page,
And friends were kind at times they might have sneered,
Which strengthened our musicianship onstage.
But still, I hate to sum up what I've done
Instead of writing something lyrical
About the way rehearsals have been run,
Or how a masterwork's a miracle.[1]
Next time, I hope that I won't be accosted
By crass prosaicism while exhausted.

---

1. That evening was our first of three performances of Haydn's Mass in C Major
"Paukenmesse" with the San Diego Symphony.

Practice Practice Practice[1]

December 6th

It is a joy to let your body do
A task it has been well-conditioned to,
For even though it may have been a while
Since it was done, your brain is versatile—
A memory, once it has been created,
With others soon will be assimilated,
And its specific time and place, in code,
Is permanently, perfectly bestowed.
When you encounter patterns that you know,
From mind to body will the memory flow
Without a conscious thought, and so a beat
Can prompt the singing voice or dancing feet.[2]
And though one can't take credit for the brain,
There's great reward from taking time to train.

1. Punchline of an old joke. Q: How do you get to Carnegie Hall? A: Practice, practice, practice! Also, the repetition led me to write the stanzas of this sonnet in couplets instead of alternating end rhymes.
2. Referring to an excellent dance class and an excellent Haydn performance.

357

Make Shift[1]

December 7th

A universal irritant is that
Which doesn't function when it is desired,
Especially when someone is left flat,
Bereft of services that are required.
Thus scrambling must commence to fill the need
To find a work-around that will augment
One's assets and, with fortune, may succeed
So well the fix becomes quite permanent.
But failure of the old, familiar guard
Makes room for different thinking in the ranks,
And while the old's not something to discard,
The new's a thing for which one can give thanks.
The question of who's better's rendered moot
By one's ability to troubleshoot.

---

1. You never notice how much you need a printer until it doesn't work when you need it.

All the Trimmings[1]

December 8th

A box of tchotchkes spanning my existence—
Some catch the light, some catch the memory,
And with the added benefit of distance,
Those ice pop sticks and yarn transcend the twee.
Worn velvet and the light-blanched colored papers
Seen through nostalgia-clouded oculi,
Will conjure thoughts of past tree-stealing capers,
With long and chilly roadside standings by.[2]
So why, if all the thoughts are cheerful ones
Appropriate to holiday tradition,
Does melancholy sit upon the fun
And try to force the joy into submission?
Regardless, I won't let what can't be brought
Overwhelm my thanks for what I've got.

---

1. On trimming the tree and decking the hall with fake evergreens. This was our first
time hanging the childhood ornaments that our parents sent to us.
2. Since my parents preferred cedars to pines as Christmas trees, my father scouted
out appropriately-sized cedars growing just off the highway and organized tree-
stealing missions under cover of darkness, which usually involved borrowing our
neighbor's pickup truck and enlisting a crew of our friends.

Imaginary Friends

December 9th

I like the thought of you, and that's enough.
I know your name and face, of course, but all
The rest is only insubstantial stuff,
Though thoroughly delightful folderol.
I like the sound of you, and that is pleasant,
Although I like to listen while alone,
And open my enjoyment like a present
With none to disapprove or to condone.
While most exuberance I freely share,
This parasocial[1] pleasure is for me—
Because it is a lopsided affair,
It's nourished by and thrives in privacy.
Yours is a wondrous counterfeit to fill
With gorgeous grist my ever-grinding mill.

---

1. Parasocial interactions, in media and communication studies, describes imagined relationship that members of an audience feel that they have with the characters or celebrities in the media they consume.

Evaluation Eve[1]

December 10th

I doubt that I shall ever like auditions,
But now I'm better able to endure
The fight or flight response, and repetitions
Beforehand and a warm-up reassure
That I am well-prepared to do my best,
And if I don't, then it was not to be—
It's ultimately pointless to protest
That failure or success was solely me.
I bring the selfsame talent to the table
Each time I lay my cards upon the felt.
Good fortune might my finest play enable
But in the end, I take what I am dealt,
I hope what skill I offer will attract
And that the deck against me isn't stacked.

---

1. I didn't get the job, but I'm really glad I went for it.

Figurative[1]

December 11th

A story on the radio compared
The storm in drought to paying off a bill
While deep in debt. Long after it had aired
That simple simile is with me still,
Because that story seemed a metaphor
For all the trying times one must endure,
For every obstacle exposes more,
Perspective shifts revealing things obscure.
Perception grows, although precision fades,
One understands the fragile film between
What is and what lurks under fancy's shades;
Unknowns that may be felt instead of seen.
We comprehend through allegory, but
Analogy's a metaphor for what?

---

1. A sonnet that attempts to figure out layers of figurative language.

362

Rain Through Windows

December 12th

Through one, I watched the dogs observe the rain
That started falling just as we returned
From misting walk to home and hearth again,
For future outings they were unconcerned.
And on the bus another, blurred by fog
Within with rain without, the route by rote
I know, as finding bearings is a slog
For those with bags strapped underneath their coats.
At night, though salty drops obscure my view
Of audience beyond proscenium,
I see the now-familiar born anew
And to the present ecstasy succumb.[1]
So welcome, showers, to this thirsty clime
You have arrived at an auspicious time.

---

1. Despite having seen *Hunchback* numerous times by that point, Michael Arden often made me cry at the end with his moving portrayal of Quasimodo.

On My Last Show[1]

December 13th

The end of any run is bittersweet—
To bid a cast, creative team, and crew,
The memories that live in voice and feet,
Tradition, set, and theater fond *adieu*
Makes one recall the joy it was to bring
To life a story that's withstood the years;
That even when through weeping one must sing,
One understands how precious are the tears.
And now that we must go our separate ways,
Though new and thrilling paths we all will roam,
As long as memory lasts, that backwards gaze,
In Notre Dame we'll always find a home.
And as the bells are struck and banners furled,
We're grateful to have been atop that world.[2]

1. Though *Hunchback of Notre Dame* ran for more performances, December 13th was
the last time my team of choristers performed.
2. Refers to one of the songs in the show, "Top of the World."

Up in the Air

December 14th

Like children with balloons who understand
The ground is deadly in the game they play
And seek to keep aloft with foot or hand
That airy sphere as long as deftness may,
I've filled my year's remaining days and nights,
With singing, learning music, and performing,
In hopes that all the caroling and lights
Will keep the clouds of grief from ever forming.
For each experience that gives me joy
Makes melancholy in an equal measure,
Enough to temporarily destroy
The satisfaction one may find in leisure.
Once more I bat myself into the air
And hope that word and song will keep me there.[1]

---

1. One way to postpone post-performance crash is to have lots of back-to-back performances. This is, however, exhausting and cannot save one from eventually having to say goodbye to a show or a piece of music.

Endurance[1]

December 15th

No matter what I do today, I find
Dissatisfaction lurking there behind,
Convincing me my throat's too sore to sing
Or that I'll be too tired for caroling,[2]
That writing is a pointless exercise,
For my ambitions meager skills outsize,
When living feels too tiresome and too rough,
The reason's that I don't work hard enough.
The only way I know to get through days
When darkness wants to drag me in its ways
Is to obtain the comforts that I crave
And to be bold enough to misbehave.
With skillful application of good beer,
Until the new year I shall persevere.

---

1. An exhausted sonnet written entirely in couplets in which it became clear that I was
not wholly successful in postponing my post-performance crash.
2. Annual caroling at O'Brien's Pub.

Wishes Are Children[1]

December 16th

For those of you whose hearts will ache tonight[2]
I wish with all of mine that you'll find peace.
For those in pain, may comfort slake tonight
Your agony, and lead to its surcease.
For those who grieve, good memories I pray,
And justice for the ranks of the oppressed,
The lonely, may joy loneliness allay,
With equilibrium for the depressed.
Is it delusion, when my cheeks grow wet,
To think I send catharsis to all nations,
Into the hearts of those I've never met
And help alleviate their tribulations?
Most likely—yet I know I'd rather err
Upon the side of empathy and care.

---

1. From Stephen Sondheim's song "Children Will Listen" from *Into the Woods.*
2. It was a disheartening day in the news: the Taliban killed over a hundred children at a military school in Pakistan; hostages were killed in a situation in Sydney; a gunman was on the loose in Pennsylvania after killing members of his family; thousands were estimated to have died from fighting in Sudan; and one of six remaining northern white rhinoceroses passed away at the San Diego Zoo's Safari Park.

Nota Bene[1]

December 17th

I crossed the street and there, stopped at the light,
A chartreuse Prius, like the one you drive,
Or drove, and in its mileage took delight
When we talked cars and you were still alive.
So, automatically I turned my head
To see if you or wife were at the wheel,
And that's when I remembered you are dead——
This fact, it seems, will always feel unreal.
But then again, I lack a mantelpiece
Where, until recently, your stocking hung.
My thoughts of you come often with caprice
And scorn for puerile music, played or sung.
Though years have passed, your lines remain distinct.
Unless erased, you'll never be extinct.

---

1. *In memoriam* n.b., or Nathan Brock, a good friend gone too soon. He passed
unexpectedly on July 17th, 2012 at the age of 35.

Pay Gap[1]

December 18th

Among creators it has long been known
That things we make have value far beyond
Their salability, and it's been shown
That such creative work creates a bond
Between all cultures, peoples, generations,
And benefits the brain in myriad ways,
Like bridging gaps in people's educations——
And yet this work is rarely work that pays.
The writing earning me my daily bread,
Repetitive, redundant, and transparent,
At least affords me clarity of head——
No public good is readily apparent.
I doubt that I shall reach across the nations
With one of my expense justifications.

---

1. A sonnet about the gap between work one would not do if not paid to do so and
work which sometimes one does for the joy of doing it.

Wassail

December 19th

The beautiful guitar I mostly-play,
Dave's flute and twelve-string, Janet's dulcet cello
And Jeff's tin whistles join, one winter's day
To lead O'Brien's Pub in merry bellow.
The words are garbled, some don't know the tune,
And calls for "Free Bird" happen frequently,
But none to Christmas carols is immune,
Especially when all are in one key.
And this is why we come from year to year,
With different leaders and with different casts
To raise a glass or three of Christmas beer
To keep tradition, hoping memory lasts.
Departed or far-flung though now we be,[1]
We're joined in time by sharing melody.

---

1. Dedicated to John "Spanky" Hanson, who organized pub caroling for many years prior to his passing and in whose memory we will always attempt to get the pub to sing "O Tannenbaum" in German.

Sum[1]

December 20th

A whole can be, as Aristotle said,
So much more than the sum of all its parts,
But if we look at *sum* itself instead,
Linguistic variation it imparts.
For starters, dim sum, when enjoyed with friends
Is so much more than lunch with tasty food,
In Latin, *sum*'s "to be," which then portends
A verb irregular and misconstrued.
And this is why our sums and our subtractions
Have multiplied as our divisions spread.
There is no function then, for mere abstractions
Accounting for those languages long dead.
Some texts were lost, but some survive unbroken,
And some words will outlast those merely spoken.

---

1. A sonnet inspired by dim sum with Corine and Sharon. Also having been exposed to Latin at an impressionable age. Also arithmetic.

In the Dark[1]

December 21st

The darkest hour is often said to be
Before the dawn, but those who know the verges
Of night and day acknowledge they will see
A lightened sky before the sun emerges.
The hour at which the night is most persistent:
That midpoint in between sun's set and rise,
As any solstice should be equidistant
From equinoctes as each season dies.
And now that I myself am just beyond
The bleakest hour of this, the longest night,
I scan the sky for signs that it has dawned
And hope that looming clouds shall sun ignite.
Obscurity I seize and find a handle
Because I choose to face it with a candle.

---

1. A winter solstice sonnet.

Setback and Forth

December 22nd

An endless litany of work demands
That's followed by the thrill of voicing song
With cherished friends and those with gifted hands,
Then followed by new music in a throng,[1]
Supplanted, then, by comprehensive mope,
Upon deliverance of lousy news[2]
About a thing for which I'd dared to hope;
Yet gentle hugs frustrations can defuse.
Discouraged, sad, and tired though I may be,
My final workday's scheduled for tomorrow
Before few precious days of liberty—
To think on that will soften any sorrow.
Tomorrow, I shall sacred songs employ.[3]
Though glad of comfort, I hold hope for joy.

---

1. That night, I had two rehearsals: a dress rehearsal for a Catholic church's Christmas concert and a rehearsal with Master Chorale for our New Year's Eve concert for the Spreckels Organ's centennial.
2. Official word came that I did not get the job for which I'd auditioned ("Evaluation Eve," December 10th).
3. We performed Johann Sebastian Bach's Cantata 30, *Freue dich, erlöste Schar*, BWV 30, and Antonio Vivaldi's less-famous but still glorious *Gloria in D major*, RV 588.

Baroque Fix

December 23rd

A day of tediousness and pointless stresses
Combined with ever-growing to-do lists,
Is one that unavoidably depresses,
Inexorable snappishness persists
Until this truly frivolous annoyance
Must needs compete for vanishing attention
Against the zenith of Baroque flamboyance;
Complexity defying comprehension.
As dark can only be destroyed by light
And hate can only be destroyed by love
Banality with Bach[1] we all shall smite,
Via Vivaldi[2] we'll raise songs above.
When days are filled with sputtering invective,
My concert nights help put things in perspective.

---

1. Cantata 30, BWV 30.
2. *Gloria in D Major,* RV 588.

The Mystery Gift

December 24th

A heavy box arrived, one surface ripped
And fearing for the worst, I looked inside,
But for the contents I was ill-equipped,
And so I held them to my chest and cried—
Two volumes, out-of-print and long desired[1]
Once added to my wish list for a lark;
A gift whose choice seems perfectly inspired,
And in that perfect moment hit its mark.
The box contained no clue as to the senders,
Though only my immediate family
Knew of my list, so there were few contenders,
And he admitted his identity.[2]
Dear brother, I wear thanks upon my sleeve
For that which I'm so lucky to receive.

---

1. *The Annotated Sherlock Holmes*, edited by William S. Baring-Gould (not to be
mistaken for Leslie S. Klinger's *The New Annotated Sherlock Holmes*, that partially
inspired my sonnet on January 2nd), which had been on my to-read list for years.
2. After I made a series of showy deductions worthy of Holmes himself (or Watson, at
the very least), my brother admitted the deed. Thanks, Pete!

Merry Little Christmas[1]

December 25th

Sometimes, a family Christmas will consist
Of sitting on the carpet with your spouse
While both of you are alternately kissed
And cuddled by the canines of the house,
And rather than a sleigh ride through the drifts,
A walk around an isthmus in the bay,[2]
Instead of six-course dinners after gifts,
A simple meal for two will do today.
Each commonplace activity gains meaning
When busy lives demand time spent apart,
So gratitude for festive intervening
In moments such as this will fill the heart.
May pride and expectation someday soften,
That we can all enjoy such things more often.

---

1. From Ralph Blane and Hugh Martin's beautifully melancholy Christmas song,
"Have Yourself a Merry Little Christmas" from the musical *Meet Me in St. Louis.*
2. Fiesta Island, the largest off-leash dog area in San Diego.

On the Feast of Stephen[1]

December 26th

Though Boxing Day has long-observed traditions,
My household has decided on our own:
A day of rest for Christmas-worn musicians
We celebrate by tuning out the phone,
Then making copious puns with cherished friends
And toasting the atrocious ones with glee.
Or being glad when water line descends
When snaking plumbing that's been clogged with tea.
Whatever rite or ritual we choose
Be it necessity or frivolous,
Enlightening or simply to amuse,
The impetus to do it came from us.
Our guiding principle is one puissant:
Enjoy the day by doing what you want.

---

1. St. Stephen's feast day is observed in the Western church on December 26th and was immortalized in John Mason Neale's lyrics for "Good King Wenceslas."

The Inspiration Game[1]

December 27th

One thing is lacking motivation when
There are a dozen things you'd rather do,
Like listen to adored comedians
Pretend to fly a man to Timbuktu.[2]
It's quite another when you'd rather write
The thoughts to form the basis of a story
And not the piece that must be done tonight,
As it occurs in mental territory—
Ideas, like rabbits, tend to reproduce
When shielded from the crush of worldly stresses,
Yet their abundant presence can't reduce
Anxieties that spring from their excesses.
Wild fancies sparked from works of great renown—
If only I had time to write them down!

1. A pun on the film *The Imitation Game*, whose star, Benedict Cumberbatch, also
stars in the BBC Radio comedy series *Cabin Pressure*.
2. Refers to the *Cabin Pressure* episode "Timbuktu."

How I Won the War[1]

December 28th

As one conversant with rhyme, verse, and scansion,
And long-familiar forms of poetry,
It's not surprising I should seek expansion
From borders of familiarity.
Though music of the spoken word's eternal,
Specific phrases and their orchestrations
Can bring about acknowledgment internal
That some things, Wilde once wrote, produce vibrations.[2]
And so when watching other tales that came
A few years after those I know too well,
They cannot but my memory inflame,
Along with pride that it was done so well.[3]
Though kismet might have lighted my ambition,
'Twas perspicacity made me audition.[4]

---

1. A 1967 black comedy based on the novel by Patrick Ryan about an inept World War II lieutenant whose platoon tries to get rid of him, but he manages to unwittingly get almost all of them killed.
2. From Oscar Wilde's *The Importance of Being Earnest*. Additional details may be found in footnote 2 of "That Rings a Bowl" (July 7th).
3. I got my husband to watch Disney's animated film *Hercules*. It came out the year after *The Hunchback of Notre Dame*.
4. It was a nice thing to recall, having had an unsuccessful audition, that I have had successful ones.

Pelican[1]

December 29th

I soar above the waves with little clearance,
As if an unseen cloak composed of breeze
From choppy waters wanting interference
Protects me over other devotees.
I rise in joyful arc into the sky,
Then turn my shoulder to the sea below
To dive upon what fodder I espy
And fill my bill, and through its grace I grow.
The ancients thought that I would pierce my breast
To feed my young, a sign of sacrifice,
But for the fish that I would fain ingest,
I'm not a coat-of-arms device.
Thus, any symbol others may exalt
I'll swallow with a goodly grain of salt.

---

1. This sonnet was inspired concurrently by seeing pelicans at the beach and by La
Jolla Playhouse, whose logo features the pelican because former Artistic Director Des
McAnuff liked the symbolism of a native bird species that now thrives after having
been endangered.

Penultimate

December 30th

Wan winter sun, the second to the last
Of this, the year I chose to sonnet daily,
Your rise announced all starts of poems past
And now, upon the end you shine so palely
Upon this concept that I'm now outlining,
Which has already set my scansion spinning
I know what words may yet survive aligning,
With confidence I lacked at the beginning.[1]
And yet I feel that I have hardly started,
Since every day's addition is discrete,
And each idea heretofore uncharted——
It's hard to see this as a single feat,
Unless it is embracing introspection,
And finding good alongside imperfection.

---

1. Unsurprisingly, one thing I've gotten pretty good at in the course of daily sonnet writing is writing sonnets.

Last, Not Least

December 31st

This is the last time I will write my life
Into a daily sonnet, those things great,
Exciting, middling, sad, and sometimes strife,
Through stubbornness one cannot understate.
Tonight, I'll sing to thousands and the sky
To fete a civic gem's centenary[1]
Then dinner, where we'll bid the year goodbye
And sonnet cycle done successfully.
Tomorrow, will I feel compelled to write,
Thus letting loose the stories in my head?
Or will those nagging feelings in the night
Inspire me to read a book instead?
To paraphrase the words of one less boring
Who knows? I'll get the sled. Let's go exploring![2]

---

1. The Spreckels Organ in Balboa Park began its centenary celebration on New Year's Eve, and I sang in a concert in its honor, including the premier of a new work by Stephen Sturk.
2. "Let's go exploring!" are the final words of Bill Watterson's comic strip, *Calvin and Hobbes.*

Addenda

This Gull Is on Fire[1]

January 6th

A common gull that flew toward the dawn
Was suddenly with pinkish orange aflame,
As lead by alchemy had undergone
Its transformation, baseness overcame.
I knew it was a trick of light, and yet
Its unexpected beauty gave me pause,
I fixed it in my mind, not to forget
The transient perfection that it was——
For who among us would not wish to be
But for an instant, thus illuminated,
That all who were so lucky as to see
Should with the memory be ever sated?
As when the sunbeams common facets gild,
Am I when I with gratitude am filled.

---

1. A pun on Alicia Keys's song "Girl on Fire," and a thank-you sonnet to those who kept me going during the sonnet project. Consider this a bonus leap-day sonnet for years that have a February 29th.

Mass for the Dead[1]

January 24th, 2017

I tried to write a verse replete
With symbols and dactylic feet
To faithfully portray my grief
That sweet Giovanni lies beneath[2]
The sandy earth where first he raced
To flush the birds he bounced and chased.
By she, whose scruff he loved to tug,
His unexpected grave was dug.[3]
But all those masses, mysteries,
and hearts,4 intended to appease
My sorrow and give shapely frame
To sadness, are but hollow claim.
Your ghost in the periphery
Of dream and waking comforts me;
When I refill your water bowl,
I feel your paw prints on my soul.

---

1. Giovanni, my scruffy muse, left us on November 4th, 2016, shortly after an enormous tumor was discovered in his chest. Though the surgeons did their best to remove the mass, which was killing him, he passed away on the operating table at the age of six years and eleven months.
2. Of course, this isn't a sonnet, since there are sixteen lines. I also relied on assonance in this couplet instead of a perfect rhyme. But it's the poem I wanted to write in Gio's memory: a hybrid for my scruffy whatsit featuring tetrameter (four feet per line) in four stanzas for my four-footed boy.
3. We took some of Gio's ashes to Fiesta Island Dog Park, a place he loved. When we found a lush, grassy spot, I started to say some halting words in gratitude for his life, when Hildegard snorted and started digging. I sprinkled Gio's ashes in the hole, the sort of which he and Hildy used to dig together.
4. I wrote an outline for a fancy sonnet a few weeks after his passing, which involved multiple definitions of each of these three symbols. But when I tried to assemble it two months later, it felt artificial and pretentious.

Acknowledgements

This book owes a debt to many, but first and foremost to my husband Jeff, who supported this project from inception to completion with his time, talent, patience, and kindness. Enormous thanks to my editor J.L. Aldis, who braved the British/American English divide with aplomb and good humo(u)r, and whose incisive comments vastly improved this text and annotations. Deep gratitude to Annie Tarbuck for her invaluable advice in preparing this manuscript. Much love to my parents, Peter C. and Ellen Weber, who dutifully read every single sonnet in raw form and still speak to me. Deserving smooches is Sara Miller, without whose encouragement/threats I might never have begun. Love to Amelia Ray and Sharon Torigoe for daily encouragement and butt-kicking when needed, and to Helen Mout, Dana Wayne, Anna Gardberg, Angie Sutherland, Mike Shearing, Petrina Walker, Delphi Psmith, Lorrie Kim, and Melissa Anderson, whose kind and thoughtful comments throughout the project were balm. Eternal love to writing campers Wendy Worthington, Lin Thornhill, Murphy McCall, Jae Enyon, Hilary Justice, Elisabeth Carnell, M.R. Glass, Annie Tarbuck, Melissa Smith, Sara Miller, Clancy Drake, and Jennifer Keller.

Special thanks to Bonjwing Lee, Az Klymiuk, Patrick "Pup Atlas" Bowman, Weston Bennett, Christine Allois, San Diego Master Chorale, San Diego Women's Chorus, San Diego Opera, SACRA/PROFANA, Downbeat Big Band, the San Diego Symphony and artistic director Jahja Ling, the Cygnet Theatre, the Old Globe Theatre, La Jolla Playhouse, Disney Theatrical Group, the Los Angeles Philharmonic, University of California San Diego, BBC Radio 4, BBC One, National Theatre Live, Michael Giacchino, Alan Menken, Stephen Schwartz, B.A. Huffman, Gary McKercher, Martin Green, Bryan Verhoye, John Russell, Juan Carlos Acosta, John and Dean Hansen-Tarbox, Krishan Oberoi, Kirsten Oberoi, Chris Allen, Kathleen Hansen, Jason Carl Rosenberg, Stephen Sturk, Massimo Zanetti, Nathan and Vicky Brock, and Audrey Evans Lee.

About the Author

Libby Weber writes and edits fiction and nonfiction and specializes in verse and lyrics. She is also a classically-trained soprano, a core singer with SACRA/PROFANA, a choral scholar at All Souls' Episcopal Church, and performs with the San Diego Master Chorale and Folklore Guild. After growing up in a log cabin in rural Illinois, she earned a theatre degree and four varsity letters in fencing from Northwestern University before moving to San Diego, where she lives with her husband and two dogs.

Twitter: @thelibbyweber
Website: www.libbyweber.com

Made in the USA
Columbia, SC
05 May 2018